From Burning TO BLUEPRINT

REBUILDING BLACK WALL STREET AFTER A CENTURY OF SILENCE

By:
Kevin L. Matthews II, M.S.

Foreword by:
Hannibal B. Johnson

Praise for From Burning to Blueprint

"Kevin Matthews II has written an insightful book on the importance of Rebuilding Black Wall Street After a Century of Silence.

As his book aptly illustrates, we need to take responsibility for the wrongs of the past and present and engage in serious conversations that can help us move forward. The first step in the recovery process is admitting a problem exists.

As a fifth-generation Oklahoman, I did not learn about the Tulsa Race Massacre until age 45 when I was appointed to the Board of University Center Tulsa - now OSU Tulsa – and discovered that the university had been built on ground where many lost their lives during the Greenwood Massacre.

Kevin tells the story of the 1921 Tulsa Race Massacre while trying to answer many of the questions he had as a child growing up just one block from the site of the massacre. He also discusses the current wealth gap that exists in our country and provides many useful ideas to make things better."

—Tom Bennett, Jr.
PhD, Chairman of the Board, First Oklahoma Bank

"Black Wall Street's destruction in Tulsa's forgotten past is crucial context for the obstacles to Black wealth today. With this insightful blueprint, it's possible to overcome these obstacles and create long-lasting wealth."

—Harlan Landes
Founder, The Plutus Foundation

Library of Congress Cataloging-in-Publication Data

Name: Matthews II, Kevin L., author.

Title: From Burning to Blueprint: Rebuilding Black Wall Street After a Century of Silence/Kevin L. Matthews II

Description: Tulsa: Kevin L. Matthews II | Includes bibliographical references and index. | Summary: "Tells the story of the 1921 Tulsa Race Massacre in the era of the Black Lives Matter movement and social activism."

Subjects: Tulsa Race Massacre | Black Lives Matter | African Americans | Oklahoma History | Race | Greenwood (Tulsa, OK) | Racism | Economics | Racial Wealth Gap | Black Wall Street |

Identifiers: LLCN 2021905343 | ISBN 978-1-7366-6670-8 (paperback) | ISBN 978-1-7366667-1-5 (ebook)

LC record available at http://lccn.loc.gov/2021905343

Book design by Marites D. Bautista

TABLE OF CONTENTS

For Carol Watson.

FOREWORD

Hannibal B. Johnson

In the early 1900s, the Black community in Tulsa, the "Greenwood District," gained national renown. Dubbed "Black Wall Street," the neighborhood teemed with entrepreneurial and business activity: professional service providers like doctors, lawyers, pharmacists, and dentists; commercial establishments like beauty parlors, barbershops, dance halls, pool halls, movie theaters, restaurants, grocery stores, and so much more. Greenwood Avenue, its nerve center, bristled with excitement and intrigue.

The 1921 Tulsa Race Massacre temporarily stilled the Greenwood District. Marauding rioters seized upon this segregated enclave, leaving in their wake death and destruction. The result: the worst incident of mass anti-Black violence in United States history.

In a remarkable resurrection, Tulsa's Black citizens rebuilt the Greenwood District from the ashes. The community peaked in the early-to-mid-1940s, boasting well over 200 Black-owned, Black-operated enterprises.

Beginning in the 1960s, changed social, political, and economic conditions at the local, state, and national levels sparked a steep downward spiral. Integration and urban renewal ranked among the chief catalysts of this marked decline.

Integration loosened the Jim Crow-imposed grip on Black dollars that kept Greenwood District businesses afloat. Urban renewal—specifically, the location of Interstate 244 that now bisects the Greenwood District—removed Black businesses and Black bodies from their homes.

Today's Black Wall Street, an integrated, collaborative community, consists of residential, commercial, artistic, educational, cultural, entertainment, and religious elements. These entities work together to reclaim part of the past glory of this special, and for some, sacred, place.

As Chair of the Education Committee for the 1921 Tulsa Massacre Centennial Commission ("Centennial Commission"), I devote considerable time to educational and curricular matters. I also serve as local curator for Greenwood Rising, the history center built by the Centennial Commission. Among the chief goals of the Centennial Commission and Greenwood Rising is sharing the complete narrative of Tulsa's Historic Greenwood District with the world.

The overarching element of that story is the triumph of the human spirit—indomitability, perseverance, and resilience. The Greenwood District originals envisioned something remarkable, brought it to fruition, witnessed its destruction, and rebuilt it from the smoldering ruins.

We must teach this history for its moral lessons, no doubt. But we must all teach it for the early examples of Black economic and entrepreneurial success it offers; for the modeling it provides. The Black Wall Street icons succeeded in places and spaces where failure seemed foreordained. Surely, then, we can surmount lesser mountains.

We must acknowledge that systemic racism exists in this country—always has. For our lifetimes, it will continue to exist, perhaps diminished, but never fully abated.

That said, the challenges that confront us today pale in comparison to those our Black Wall Street forebears faced. Nevertheless, they achieved. The economic and entrepreneurial legacy they left should place us in the no-fear zone.

We must continue to chip away at systemic racism while we simultaneously seize our rightful places in the economic sphere *despite the artificial barriers we face*. That is the Black Wall Street Mindset.

The Black Wall Street Mindset is a mental construct predicated on the indomitable human spirit exhibited by the titans of Tulsa's Historic Greenwood District—people like J.B. Stradford (attorney and hotelier); Mabel B. Little (beautician and community activist); A.J. Smitherman (journalist and civil rights activist); O.W. Gurley (businessman and developer); Simon Berry (transportation entrepreneur and hotelier); John & Loula Williams (business owners of multiple enterprises); and Mary Elizabeth Jones Parrish (journalist and author).

The Black Wall Street Mindset is malleable and portable; agile and not moored to any specific geographic area, though inspired by the Black Wall Street originals. It is not constrained by limiting social conditions like Jim Crow segregation the founders of the Greenwood District faced. Its reach is global; universal.

Kevin L. Matthews II, the son of an entrepreneur, is a former financial advisor. He wrote this book, *From Burning to Blueprint: Rebuilding Black Wall Street After a Century of Silence*, to share insights and guidance about Black engagement in the economic arena, both individually and collectively. Black Wall Street is his inspiration.

Matthews implores us to recognize Black spending power and savings potential. He challenges us to create, grow, and protect Black wealth. He counsels us to invest knowledgeably and prudently.

Matthews' work suggests Black economic and entrepreneurial prowess—the Black Wall Street Mindset—is the *sine qua non* of Black progress. The way forward involves expanding the Black bourgeoisie in ways that reaffirm cultural connections and reassert demands for social, political, and economic justice throughout American society.

We are the progeny of Black Wall Street legends. We are heirs to a proud tradition of economic and entrepreneurial excellence. Let us be the kings and queens of commerce we were meant to be.

*****

Hannibal B. Johnson, a Harvard Law School graduate, is an author, attorney, and consultant. He has taught at The University of Tulsa College of Law, Oklahoma State University, and The University of Oklahoma. Johnson serves on numerous boards and commissions, including the federal 400 Years of African-American History Commission and the 1921 Tulsa Race Massacre Centennial Commission. His books, including *Black Wall Street 100: An American City Grapples With Its Historical Racial Trauma*, chronicle the African American experience in Oklahoma and its indelible impact on American history. Johnson's play, *Big Mama Speaks—A Tulsa Race Riot Survivor's Story*, was selected for the 2011 National Black Theatre Festival and has been staged in Caux, Switzerland. He has received copious honors and awards for this work and community service.

PREFACE

The twenty-four hours between May 31 and June 1, 1921 set the backdrop and context for my childhood. During that time frame, five hotels, thirty-one restaurants, eight doctors' offices, and two movie theaters were reduced to ash. Nearly three hundred people were killed. This event became known as the 1921 Tulsa Race "Riot," one of the worst acts of domestic terrorism in the United States. In short, it was a massacre, not a riot, one that left a stain in the city for nearly a century. Prior to this attack, the Greenwood District in Tulsa, Oklahoma, was known as Black Wall Street and it was among the wealthiest Black communities in the nation.

Today, nearly one hundred years later, there are less than five grocery stores, zero movie theaters, zero Black-owned hotels, and zero hospitals. To date, many of the bodies still haven't been found. This is a chapter in history that most Tulsans, like me, learned about via whispers between old folks and almost never in a formal classroom setting, despite going to school on Greenwood Avenue.

For most of my life, no one intentionally traveled to Tulsa. You were either lucky enough to escape the area or it was the unnecessary layover stop on your flight, a city long removed from its status as the Oil Capital of the World. When I was growing up, Tulsa was a middle child of sorts—not big enough to feel like a "real city," not small enough to be a cozy oasis, but it was home. Yet over the past few years, Tulsa has suddenly become a destination. At one point it was ranked by Forbes as one of the best cities to start a business. As the massacre's centennial approaches, dozens have swooped in to try and memorialize, and in some cases capitalize, on our legacy and pain. Many of these projects are welcomed and needed, but so too are the stories of those who have lived in the shadows of the massacre, those still left with its ashes and questions. While we may not say it out loud, we do ask silently, "Where were you ten years ago, before Tulsa and the 1921 massacre was popular, before it was a plot point in HBO's *Watchmen* or *Lovecraft Country*? What's going to happen once the cameras leave and the 'moment' passes?"

While I'm not the only person who feels a kinship with Black Wall Street, I do feel uniquely positioned to tell this story. After all, it was Booker T. Washington who called the Greenwood District the "Black Wall Street of America." Ironically, in 2008, I graduated from Booker T. Washington High School and went on to Hampton University, the same school Washington himself graduated from in 1875.

Between 2015 and 2019, there was a boom in ancestry DNA kits. Those who took the tests were often overjoyed with the results that they received. They had the opportunity to learn about their family history and legacy and in what areas they may have relatives. In contrast, for me, learning about the 1921 Tulsa Race Massacre brought pain and confusion. A century's legacy was completely hidden and overlooked, literally buried in my own backyard in unmarked graves.

It's difficult to describe the type of confusion you feel when someone else has to explain your own history to you. I felt a certain embarrassment each time someone taught me something new about what happened during those pivotal twenty-four hours in the Greenwood District. Because the massacre wasn't a point of emphasis within my city or school system, I had no idea that anyone would have heard of the incident beyond city limits. Ironically, I found myself learning more about what happened in Tulsa when I was thousands of miles away from Tulsa. In fact, learning about the massacre helped me make my college decision.

During spring break in 2007, Booker T. Washington HS launched its first HBCU tour. It was also the first time I would travel out of the state to see other historically Black colleges (The state of Oklahoma has only one historically Black university). Of the seven colleges we visited, Hampton University stood out most, but not because of the campus or the subjects I wanted to study. My tour guide was from Tulsa, and she talked about all the things she learned about the massacre during her time at Hampton. She taught me more in thirty minutes than I'd learned in seventeen years living one block away from Greenwood Ave.

What happened one hundred years ago still plagues the Greenwood District and North Tulsa as a whole. The city continues to be highly segregated today; North Tulsa makes up 17 percent of the city's total population but is over 80 percent Black.[1] In 2014, Tulsa ranked within the top 20 cities for national income inequality.[2] Finally, 35 percent of north Tulsa's population lives in poverty compared to 17 percent in the rest of the city.[3] How did the same area that was once home to the center of Black wealth inherit such a deficit in wealth and prosperity a century later? What set the

---

[1] Root, "HWR: Policing, Poverty and Racial Inequality in Tulsa, Oklahoma."

[2] Stancavage, "Tulsa ranks 18th in Income Inequality."

[3] Root, "HWR: Policing, Poverty and Racial Inequality in Tulsa, Oklahoma."

stage for the Tulsa Race Massacre in 1921 and what happened in the years and decades that followed?

My goal for this book is to not only tell the story of the 1921 Tulsa Race Massacre but to answer many of the questions that I had when I was a kid growing up here. Why didn't people rebuild? Why did it take so long for me and others to learn about this tragedy? And what would it take to truly rebuild a modern version of Black Wall Street today? To answer many of these questions, I've split this book into two sections. The first discusses how the stage was set for the Tulsa Massacre and the ensuing, devastating legacy. The second section discusses the current wealth divide and puts forth a roadmap to create, grow, and transfer Black wealth in a modern context.

PART I:
THE MASSACRE

INTRODUCTION

Shortly after visiting Tulsa, OK, for a campaign rally, President Donald Trump gave a speech on July 3, 2020 in the shadow of Mount Rushmore. Nearly eight minutes into his speech, he said, "Our nation is witnessing a merciless campaign to wipe out our history, defame our heroes, erase our values, and indoctrinate our children." This brand of irony is uniquely American, one that has the DNA and footprints of white supremacy stamped all around it. He was referring to the national outcry to change the names of US military bases that were named after Confederate officers and leaders and the (sometimes forceful) removal of Confederate statues. Momentum for the removal of these symbols has been around for years, but they were accelerated in 2015 when Dylann Roof, a white man, killed nine people in the historic Emanuel AME Church in Charleston, South Carolina. All of the victims were Black. Days after his capture, a website owned by Roof was discovered where he was found posing with Confederate flags and other white supremacist symbols.

The cries to remove these symbols and also end police brutality flared up again after the murder of George Floyd, a Black man in Minneapolis killed on camera on May 25, 2020. Floyd was arrested by the Minneapolis police after a convenience store employee called 911, alleging Floyd paid with a counterfeit twenty-dollar bill. The encounter ended with Derek Chauvin's left knee on the neck of

George Floyd for nearly eight minutes and forty-six seconds as he called for his mother, who died two years prior. These tensions were further sparked by the death of Breonna Taylor, a Black woman who was killed while sleeping in her own home in Louisville, Kentucky, on March 13, 2020 during a police raid. However, the incident didn't gain national attention until May 2020 due to increased attention on police brutality from celebrities and athletes. Months later, in September 2020, only one officer, Brett Hankinson, was indicted. But he wasn't indicted for killing Taylor; Hankinson was charged not for the bullets that entered her body but with "wanton endangerment" for the bullets that went through the walls and into her neighbor's apartment. To some, Hankinson was essentially charged for the bullets that missed, yet another display of how the justice system values Black lives.

Without a doubt, when the eleven states seceded from the Union between 1860 and 1861 to form the Confederacy, they fought to preserve the institution of slavery. The seceding states made this crystal clear in their declarations during the Civil War. The state of Mississippi wrote the following: "Our position is thoroughly identified with the institution of slavery—the greatest material interest of the world." Louisiana added, "The people of the slave holding States are bound together by the same necessity and determination to preserve African slavery." Texas, Georgia, South Carolina, and Virginia all echoed these sentiments.[4]

President Trump claimed that there was a campaign to "wipe out our nation's history and indoctrinate our children" by simply telling the truth about what the Confederacy obviously stood for.

---

[4] American Battlefield Trust, "The Declaration of Causes of Seceding States."

Trump, however, was contributing to his own campaign to soften the reality of how white people looted, stole, and killed their way from sea to shining sea.

It was the "Lost Cause" narrative that found its way into southern history textbooks that framed the Civil War as a heroic effort for states' rights and southern heritage. It also claimed that slavery wasn't the root cause of the war. These tenets still hold strong; a 2011 study by the Pew Research Center found that 48 percent of Americans think the Civil War was mainly about states' rights.[5]

Why and how did this alternative history of the Civil War come to exist? A part of it can be attributed to how our nation's leaders dealt with the Confederacy after the war. In a 2020 interview with *The Washington Post*, former president of the Museum of the Confederacy Waite Rawls says, "Civil wars usually end with the losers going to the hangman's noose, the guillotine, to exile or something, and in this case they just went home."[6] Lincoln would go on to issue more than sixty pardons for war-related offenses, including seventeen for treason, twelve for rebellion, and nine for holding office under the Confederacy.[7] To make matters worse, all Confederate soldiers received presidential pardons by December 25, 1868 by President Andrew Johnson, who was from Tennessee. These men (and eventually their wives and daughters) were able to go back and essentially write their own twisted version of history to cope with their losses. With the help of organizations like the United Daughters

---

[5] Heimlich, "What Caused the Civil War."

[6] The Washington Post, "How the 'Lost Cause' Narrative Became American History."

[7] Glass, "All Confederate Soldiers Gain Presidential Pardons."

of the Confederacy and Confederate Memorial Literacy Society, they quickly built monuments, created textbook committees, and pressured schoolboards to bend and soften the truth.

This would not be the only time where history was rewritten. With just two days left in his presidency, Donald Trump released *The 1776 Report* on Martin Luther King Jr. Day in 2021. It was a direct response to the award-winning *New York Times* 1619 Project that "Reframes American history around the consequences of slavery in the contributions of Black Americans."[8] In September 2020, Trump claimed that the 1619 Project was an attempt to rewrite history and teach children that "we were founded on the principle of oppression, not freedom."[9] *The 1776 Report* featured a grand total of zero professional historians and no academic footnotes or notations, making a number of sweeping defenses to justify the history of white supremacy in the United States. Among the most egregious was the claim that America's founders weren't hypocrites when advocating for civil equality even though they owned slaves.

To prove that the founding fathers weren't hypocrites on the subject of slavery, Trump's *1776 Report* tells the story of James Madison. The report says, "James Madison saw to it at the Constitutional Convention that, even when the Constitution compromised with slavery, it never used the word 'slave' to do so. No mere semantics, he insisted that it was 'wrong to admit in the Constitution the idea that there could be property in men.'"[10]

[8] Crowley and Schuessler, "Trump's 1776 Commission Critiques Liberalism."

[9] Watson and Segers, "Trump Blasts 1619 Project."

[10] The President's Advisory 1776 Commission, "The 1776 Report."

This is a dangerous and glaring omission of what actually happened with James Madison. When Madison had the power to impact policy, he never actually followed through on any of his antislavery views. In February 1801, James Madison Sr. died, leaving James Madison, the oldest son, with more than one hundred slaves. When Madison was appointed secretary of state to Thomas Jefferson, he took no steps to free those he enslaved. By 1809, when Madison became the fourth president of the United States, he brought enslaved people to serve him in the White House.

Jefferson and Madison would not be isolated cases. The United States has a well-documented, oft-ignored history of racial injustice. When Donald Trump spoke about wiping out history and erasing values, he did so while speaking on stolen land, land onto which the United States literally carved their faces. In 1868, the US signed an agreement that this land would remain a part of the Sioux Nation. When gold was found six years later, the US took the land back. It wasn't until 1980 that the Supreme Court ruled this unconstitutional and required the US to provide compensation. This compensation, now worth over $1.3 billion, is still on hold at the US Treasury today.[11] The Sioux refuse to take the money for two reasons: First, their land was never for sale. For them it was never about the money, it was about the land. Second, the money that was offered is only a fraction of the value that was extracted from the region in gold, timber, and minerals. Offering only $1 billion after more than 140 years of theft is a slap in the face.

In Tulsa, Trump continued to erase and diminish history in favor of propping up and defending white supremacy. In the middle of

[11] Streshinsky, "Saying No to $1 Billion."

a global pandemic, Trump chose Tulsa as the location for his first campaign rally since the COVID-19 crisis began. He didn't need to stop in Oklahoma, but it was the only state in the Union where he won every single county. The rally was initially scheduled for Friday, June 19, 2020, which is Juneteenth. On that day in 1865, Gen. Gordon Granger arrived in Galveston, Texas, to announce that the Civil War had ended and that all of the enslaved were free. This was two years after the Emancipation Proclamation was put forth.[12]

After pressure mounted, the Trump rally was pushed back one day to June 20. In yet another entry into a long list of lies, he then claimed that he made Juneteenth "very famous" because of his rally.[13] This completely erases the fact that Black people have been celebrating Juneteenth for decades and that it was deemed a state holiday in Texas starting in 1980.[14] Still, the president chose Tulsa, the site of the nation's most horrific attack on Black people, just three weeks after the ninety-ninth anniversary of the massacre and one day removed from a Black holiday signifying the true end of chattel slavery.

The story of the Tulsa Race Massacre follows many of the exact same patterns: theft, denial, violence, erasure. This is a merciless campaign indeed, but is not a new one.

---

[12] Silva, "What to Know about Juneteenth, the Emancipation Holiday."

[13] Chalfant, "Trump Says He Made Juneteenth 'Very Famous'."

[14] Texas State Library and Archives Commission, "Juneteenth."

CHAPTER 1:

BEFORE THE SMOKE

On Sundays, my dad would take me and my brother on after-church rides. My father, a Tulsa firefighter, knew the ins and outs of how the city was laid out. He would always make it a point to teach us something about the region as we drove. The (Frisco) railroad tracks were the original dividing line between north and south and Main Street was the dividing line for east and west. The streets to the east were named after cities east of the Mississippi River in alphabetical order; Boston Avenue, Cincinnati Avenue (later renamed Martin Luther King Jr. Boulevard.), and Detroit Avenue. And to the west, Cheyenne Avenue, Denver Avenue, Olympia Avenue, and Phoenix Avenue.

Greenwood Avenue was most likely named after Greenwood, Arkansas, or Greenwood, Mississippi.[15] Some historians lean toward Greenwood, Mississippi, as inspiration for the naming of the street since many of the first Black residents were from there. It was important to my dad that we always knew where we were in the world, how we got there, and how to find our way back home.

On the road leading up to the massacre, it's important to understand how we got there and what contributed to the

[15] Krehbiel, *Tulsa 1921*, 20.

environment that allowed such violence to occur. Most discussions about the 1921 Tulsa Race Massacre begin with an encounter between Black shoe-shiner Dick Rowland and white elevator operator Sarah Page on May 30, 1921. Beginning the story here does nothing but oversimplify and water down the true intent of white Tulsans at the time and removes the historical context of the era. It was not a misunderstanding on a hot summer day that resulted in a riot; it was a coordinated attack stoked by racial animosity among whites, an animosity gaslit by Tulsa's newspapers.

To understand this, you need to go back to the 1830s. When the Creeks and Cherokees were pushed out of their land as a part of the Trail of Tears, some of them were slave owners and settled in much of what is now Tulsa. After emancipation, the Black community began establishing themselves in the area and surrounding states. Black people were looking to escape the South and find a better environment to live and work. During the 1870s and '80s, many attempted to move to Kansas, but due to harsh weather conditions, most turned south to what was then Oklahoma territory.[16] Prior to Oklahoma's statehood in 1907, Black people living in the territory often enjoyed greater privileges then they did in the South or North. This privilege, however, did not go unnoticed by white people.

A March 1, 1890 article in *The New York Times* states: "If the Black population could be distributed evenly over the United States, it would not constitute a social or political danger. But an exclusively or overwhelmingly Negro settlement in any part of the country is, to all intents and purposes, a camp of savages."[17]

---

[16] Hirsch, *Riot and Remembrance*, 32.

[17] Hirsch, *Riot and Remembrance*, 33.

Award-winning author and journalist Ta-Nehisi Coates argues in his book *We Were Eight Years in Power* that it is not the Black gangster or rioter that strikes terror in white America. What the country really fears is "Good Negro Government."

> When it becomes clear that Good Negro Government might, in any way, empower actual Negroes over whites, then the fear sets in, the affirmative-action charges begin, and birtherism emerges. And this is because, at its core, those American myths have never been colorless. They cannot be extricated from the "whole theory slavery," which holds that an entire class of people carry peonage in their blood.[18]

As Tulsa grew, the fear of Black success and empowerment festered. The U.S. Census in 1910 had Tulsa's population at 18,182, making it the third largest city in the state behind Oklahoma City and Muskogee.[19] By 1920, Tulsa exploded to more than 72,000 residents, putting it on par with San Diego, California, and Wichita, Kansas, and there were some city directory estimates that had the population at 98,874.[20] Much of this growth was due to oil found in the surrounding areas. Going back as far as 1897, petroleum had been discovered fifty miles north of Tulsa near Bartlesville. Between 1900 and 1910, oil was being discovered across the southwest. One of the largest oil fields was found through the discovery well, Ida Glenn Number One, less than fifteen minutes south of Tulsa

---

[18] Coates, *We Were Eight Years in Power: An American Tragedy*, xv.

[19] Bureau of the Census, "*Statistics for Oklahoma*," 5.

[20] Ellsworth, *Death in a Promised Land*, 9.

in 1905. Glenpool, as it became known, was producing eighty-five barrels of oil each day by 1906, according to the Oklahoma Historical Society.[21] These numbers would continue to grow with new oil discoveries. By the time Oklahoma reached statehood in 1907, it was the nation's largest oil producer; by 1915, the state was producing 300,000 barrels of oil per day.[22] More than 120 of these oil companies had offices in Tulsa, which positioned itself as the Oil Capital of the World.

As oil fields spung up across Oklahoma, J.B Stradford, who moved to Tulsa in 1899 from Kentucky, and O.W. Gurley from Arkansas believed that Black people had more power in pooling together their resources. Both Gurley and Stradford began buying tracts of land north of the Frisco railroad tracks and only selling them to Black people around 1905. The two men had different philosophies regarding the advancement of Black people. Gurley subscribed more to Booker T. Washington's ideas while Stradford took after W.E.B. Du Bois; their contrasting views may have played a role in how each of the men responded to the attack. Gurley started his career as a teacher before taking a job with the US Postal Service. He sold his land in Perry, Oklahoma, after hearing about oil fields near Tulsa in 1905.[23] Gurley moved, going on to build boarding houses and a grocery store before opening a school. He later launched the Gurley Hotel, which was valued at $55,000 and rivaled the best white hotels in the up-and-coming city.[24]

---

[21] Oklahoma Historical Society, "Ida Glenn Number One."

[22] Ellsworth, *Death in a Promised Land*, 9-10.

[23] Gara, "The Bezos of Black Wall Street."

[24] Wills, *Black Fortunes*, 195.

Gurley's power and influence would grow as the oil industry continued to boom in Tulsa. He would own nearly half of Greenwood, collecting more than $68,000 (in 2018 dollars) in monthly rent from residents and shopkeepers.[25] By 1914, Gurley was reportedly worth $3.6 million in today's dollars and used his wealth to push back against voter suppression efforts. He also became a deputy to the Tulsa sheriff with the responsibility of serving Greenwood's Black population.[26]

Stradford, a graduate of Oberlin College and Indiana Law School, was much more direct in his dealings with white people. He once beat a white man for making negative remarks about his dark skin in the street in 1909. In 1918, he helped deter a white lynch mob in Bristow, OK, by organizing an armed group of Black men. Like Gurley, Stradford's most prominent asset was a hotel valued at $75,000, or nearly $2.5 million as of 2020. The Stradford Hotel, located on 301 N. Greenwood Avenue. was at one point the largest Black-owned hotel in America.[27] But Gurley would not be outdone. Gurley reportedly fought off three white men who entered his hotel and harassed his wife. This was a turning point for O.W. Gurley and Greenwood. Author Shomari Wills added, "If the racial conservative Gurley had resorted to using violence against whites, was there any hope of lasting peace between Greenwood and white Tulsa?"[28] We would get that answer as the population grew.

---

[25] Wills, *Black Fortunes*, 243.

[26] Wills, *Black Fortunes*, 195.

[27] Gara, "The Bezos of Black Wall Street."

[28] Wills, *Black Fortunes*, 21.

The Black population surged between 1910 and 1920, from 1,959 to 8,873, and the percentage of Tulsa's Black population increased from about 10 to 12 percent.[29] The center of this new district was Greenwood Avenue.

This growth was not ignored by white people. A story in *The Tulsa Democrat* in April of 1912 featured a headline, "Shall Tulsa be Muskogeeized?" (Muskogee at the time was known for having a high number of Black residents, just fifty miles southeast of Tulsa.) One line in that paper stated the following: "Tulsa appears now to be in danger of losing its prestige as the whitest town in Oklahoma."[30] Four years later in 1916, the city of Tulsa passed their first segregation law, which forbade people of either race from residing on any block where three quarters or more of the residents were of the other race.[31]

While the Black community was virtually shut out of the oil industry at this time, Greenwood still benefited indirectly. Those who did domestic work for white oil families were highly paid. Greenwood was also known to be a place for gambling, drinking, and other illicit pleasures which pulled in money from white people. At this point, Greenwood was *tolerated*, and white people were too busy making money to be worried about "putting Blacks in their place."[32]

This changed with the recession of 1920 after the end of World War I. Veterans, both Black and white, had difficulty integrating

[29] Hirsch, *Riot and Remembrance*, 38.

[30] Hirsch, *Riot and Remembrance*, 38.

[31] Hirsch, *Riot and Remembrance*, 41.

[32] Ellsworth, *Death in a Promised Land*, 31.

back into the economy. The country was struggling to shift away from wartime production, which caused many factories to close. In addition to that, the world was still dealing with the 1918 Spanish flu pandemic, which further slowed any hopes of a recovery. From 1919-1920, corporate profits fell 90 percent and bankruptcies tripled.[33] In Oklahoma, oil production was down 60 percent.

WWI also had residual effects in the minds of white people across the country as Black men came back to the states with a sense of pride and tangible skills in organization and mobilization, which set the stage for the Red Summer of 1919. The term "red summer" was coined by James Weldon Johnson, the man who wrote the Black national anthem, "Lift Every Voice and Sing," in 1900. In 1919, he was an NAACP field secretary and used the phrase to recognize the bloodshed underway.

As a result of the war, Black military personnel knew what it was like to fight and win, and they also saw the world beyond Jim Crow. Black soldiers were exposed for the first time overseas to a social structure that treated them differently, without the context and burden of lynching and the KKK as a constant threat. W.E.B. Du Bois crystallized these emotions when the Harlem Hellfighters returned. In 1919 he wrote, "We return fighting. Make way for democracy! We saved it in France . . . and we will save it in the United States of America." The Hellfighters spent more time in combat than any other American unit and showed the world the power of Black men in the military. But the United States worked quickly to sabotage any pride and empowerment from the war. Colonel J.L.A. Linard signed a memo published in 1919 citing

[33] Krehbiel, *Tulsa* 1921, 17.

concerns that Black soldiers and officers working with the French were being treated with too much "familiarity and indulgence" and wanted the French to institute some form of Jim Crow to prevent Black soldiers from coming home and expecting equality.

In Tulsa, many, including Southern Methodist preacher Reverend Harold Cooke, would go on to blame the race massacre on the fact that Black men were allowed to serve during WWI. He said that the leading cause of the riot was that the US government recognized them as soldiers on the same plane as white soldiers.[34] The Equal Justice Initiative in their report cited the following in reference to Black WWI veterans: "Because of their military service, Black veterans were seen as a particular threat to Jim Crow."[35]

The 380,000 Black veterans who'd returned from the war were much more equipped to defend themselves against lynching and other attacks. This was done by forming self-defense organizations in times of crisis. In July 1919 for instance, Black veterans took to the rooftops to defend their neighborhoods in Washington, DC, from white mobs.[36] Around the same time that Black soldiers returned, the Great Migration was already taking place. During the same time as Tulsa's growth between 1910-1920, the Black population in Chicago grew by 148 percent and Philadelphia's Black population grew by 500 percent, which further exacerbated white anxiety.[37] Between April and November of 1919, nearly twenty-

---

[34] Krehbiel, *Tulsa 1921*, 90.

[35] EJI, "Lynching in America."

[36] History, "Red Summer of 1919."

[37] History, "Red Summer of 1919."

five white supremacist attacks dotted the country from Omaha to Washington, DC, from Chicago to Atlanta, from New Orleans to New York City.

Each of these violent conflicts followed a similar template: As Black people discovered their power and made progress economically and politically, something would be used as a spark and fan the flames of racial fear and hysteria. This spark was often related to fears of Black men sexually assaulting white women. A bloody conflict would occur which resulted in white people "restoring order," leaving Black people to pick up the pieces and the dead and try to recover. It's also important to note that between 1900 and 1920, the majority of Confederate monuments began appearing across the South.

One could argue that Tulsa was the capstone event for these attacks, but outside of national factors that led to racial tensions, African Americans in Tulsa were dealing with two additional events.

First was the bombing carried out by the Industrial Workers of the World (IWW) on October 29, 1917. The IWW, also known as "Wobblies," was a radical labor union and, in the eyes of wealthy oilmen in Tulsa, an economic threat. Eleven IWW members were arrested at their headquarters on the corner of Brady and Main streets on November 5th and later fined by the judge T.D. Evans, who suggested that the men leave town. Police loaded the men into three cars but were ambushed by the Knights of Liberty. The Knights, described by the *Tulsa World* as the new Ku Klux Klan, flogged the men and also applied hot tar and feathers to their bodies. The Tulsa police took no actions against the Knights of Liberty. *The Tulsa Democrat* added this statement of approval about the incident: "The men of the oil fields—the loyal Americans—must take the matter into their own hands."[38]

The second event occurred in August 1920, involving a twenty-five-year-old white taxi driver named Homer Nida. Nida picked up two men and one woman outside of the Hotel Tulsa en route to Red Fork. The driver became suspicious of the passengers and pulled over at a gas station where he hid some of the money he was carrying.[39] Nida was then shot in the stomach by one of the passengers and left on the side of the road. He was later found by a garage owner who rushed him to the hospital, where Nida told the police what happened. Eighteen-year-old Roy Belton, one of the passengers, also white, was arrested and reportedly confessed, claiming that the shooting was an accident. This ordeal was played out in front of the newspaper media. When word got around that Nida died a few days later, a masked crowd assembled at the courthouse where he was being held. The men disarmed the sheriff and demanded that the guards release Belton. The men then took Belton, arms still tied, and placed him in Nida's cab, which was also stolen from the police. The crowd went to Jenks, a community just a few miles south of Tulsa, and continued to surge in number. There were at least two uniformed police officers there to keep the mob under control. One report found that police were directing traffic. Author of *Riot and Remembrance*, James S. Hirsch, uncovered a *Tulsa Tribune* article that noted the scene: ". . . perhaps for the first time in history [a city] was presented

[38] Hirsch, *Riot and Remembrance*, 64.

[39] Hirsch, *Riot and Remembrance*, 65.

with the spectacle of the written law's guardians acting tacitly in co-operation with a lynch mob."[40]

Belton's body was hanging for eleven minutes before he was cut down. The rope used to take his life was sold for fifty cents an inch. No one was punished or reprimanded. Sheriff Woolley, the man who failed to keep Roy Belton safe in custody, was quoted as saying, "I believe that Belton's lynching proved more beneficial . . . It shows to criminals that the Tulsa Men mean business."[41]

The message was loud and clear: The Tulsa police were not able to prevent a lynching from happening. If a mob could kidnap and kill a white prisoner, then no Black person would ever be safe in custody and the Black community knew this. A.J. Smitherman, the editor of the Black-owned *Tulsa Star*, said, "It is quite evident that the proper time to afford protection to any prisoner is before and not during the time he is being lynched."

The Greenwood District watched each of these events unfold: the flogging in Tulsa in 1917, the Red Summer of 1919 across the country, and the lynching of a white man in Tulsa in 1920. Should a Black man be accused or threatened by a mob, it was clear that he would need protection and that the police wouldn't guarantee anyone's safety. This forced Black Tulsans to prepare for self-defense. Any requests to trust the legal process or the authorities in general had already been overdrawn. At this point, it would be reasonable to assume that no Black person in Tulsa or across the nation had a reason to believe that justice and due process would

[40] Hirsch, *Riot and Remembrance*, 68.
[41] Ibid., 69.

ever apply to them. If the law was an inadequate tool to protect Black communities from lynch mobs, then self-defense would have to be relied upon.

> "For three centuries we have suffered and cowered . . . Today we raise the terrible weapon of Self-Defense. When the murderer comes, he shall no longer strike us in the back. When the armed lynchers gather, we too must gather armed. When the mob moves, we propose to meet it with bricks and clubs and guns.
>
> If the United States is to be a Land of Law, we would live humbly and peaceably in it—working, singing, learning and dreaming to make it and ourselves nobler and better: if it is to be a Land of Mobs and Lynchers, we might as well die today as tomorrow."

-W.E.B. Du Bois
"Let Us Reason Together," *The Crisis* 18 (September 1919): 231

Du Bois's words in 1919 accurately captured the frustration and fear that had been brewing with regard to law enforcement and lynching in Tulsa since 1917. It would not be long before the working and singing would stop and "that terrible weapon of self-defense" would be raised.

CHAPTER 2:

THE SPARK

In 1913, educator and founder of the National Negro Business League, Booker T. Washington, came to Tulsa's Greenwood District. He witnessed the thirty-five square blocks of Black-owned hotels, drug stores, grocery stores, and restaurants thriving in an era where sharecropping and convict leasing were the norm across the South.

Black Wall Street though was much more of a Black Main Street as it didn't have any true financial institutions or community anchors like a Durham, North Carolina, which also took on the moniker of Black Wall Street but with less national prominence. Durham was anchored by Mechanics and Farmers Bank, founded in 1907, and North Carolina Mutual Life Insurance Company, founded in 1898; both still exist today. Flanking Durham's Black Wall Street were several historically Black colleges and universities (HBCUs), which supplied the town with a constant stream of young talent. Shaw University was founded in 1865, North Carolina A&T State University, 1891, Winston-Salem State University, 1892, and North Carolina Central University, 1910.

Tulsa's Black Wall Street, much like the city itself, was positioned to benefit from the oil boom. There were two reasons why Tulsa's Black

Wall Street was successful. First, oil money provided opportunities for higher-paying jobs instead of the common predatory jobs that existed in the South at the time. Second, residents in the Greenwood District took pride in spending money in their own community and did so with intent. In fact, the few white people who owned businesses in Greenwood would complain that their potential Black customers were intimidated into not spending money at their businesses.[42] The stage was set: Greenwood had an entrepreneurial Black middle class that took pride in spending money with their own.

Monday, May 30, 1921

It's Memorial Day. Dick Rowland, also known as "Diamond Dick," is a shoe-shiner and delivery man. Nineteen-year-old Rowland, who dropped out of high school, is heading to the third floor of the Drexel Building at 319 South Main Street. The reason that he would head to the Drexel on a holiday is unknown. He could have simply wanted to use the restroom or deliver a package, but again, most of the offices would have presumably been closed. In the elevator of the building, he meets Sarah Page, a seventeen-year-old white woman from Kansas City who works as an elevator operator at the Drexel. No one knows exactly what happened in the elevator. Some say that Rowland tripped while entering the elevator and bumped Page, causing her to scream; this has been the most common iteration of the story. There are other versions that claim Page and Roland were in a relationship. And perhaps the less commonly held notion is that Page was a prostitute and Rowland

[42] Krehbiel, *Tulsa* 1921, 25.

was her pimp. There's also speculation that the ensuing attack was an attempt to grab real estate and "put the negro back in his place" as seen two years earlier in the Red Summer of 1919.

Randy Krehbeil, author of *Tulsa 1921*, offers this thought:

> "These questions play into a parallel narrative, one in which all that followed was not about race but about real estate; a scheme in which Whites and Blacks conspired to create a pretext for turning Greenwood into a warehouse district . . . Certainly an effort was made to exploit the riot for that purpose. Whether the riot was planned and instigated towards that end is a more sinister mystery that may never be definitively solved."[43]

Setting speculation aside, we do know this: Dick Rowland was accused of sexual assault of a white woman in broad daylight. Rowland was arrested the next day, May 31, 1921, and taken to the top floor of the courthouse, the same place that Roy Belton was abducted by the mob. That same day *The Tulsa Tribune* began instigating the underlying racial tension, fear, and frustration that whites in the city had been holding onto for years.

On May 31, 1921, one of the paper's headlines read: "Nab Negro for Attacking Girl in an Elevator." The ensuing story read:

> A negro delivery boy who gave his name to the public as "Diamond Dick" but who has been identified as Dick Rowland, was arrested on South Greenwood Avenue this

[43] Krehbiel, *Tulsa* 1921, 31.

> morning by Officers Carmichael and Pack, charged with attempting to assault the 17-year-old white elevator girl in the Drexel building early yesterday.
>
> He will be tried in municipal court this afternoon on a state charge.
>
> The girl said she noticed the negro a few minutes before the attempted assault looking up and down the hallway on the third floor of the Drexel building as if to see if there was anyone in sight but thought nothing of it at the time.
>
> A few minutes later he entered the elevator she claimed, and attacked her, scratching her hands and face and tearing her clothes. Her screams brought a clerk from Renberg's store to her assistance and the negro fled. He was captured and identified this morning both by the girl and the clerk, police say.
>
> Tenants of the Drexel building said the girl is an orphan who works as an elevator operator to pay her way through business college.[44]

The Tulsa Tribune was widely blamed for being the spark that started the massacre. However, it was not this article alone that was a call to action for white mobs with the propensity to enforce their version of justice. Many over the years have also cited an article from the *Tribune* with the title "To Lynch a Negro Tonight" as being an even bigger reason for the conflict, the one that encouraged whites to gather at the courthouse. That article has not been located; copies

[44] The Tulsa Tribune, "Nab Negro for Attacking Girl in an Elevator."

of the *Tribune* were microfilmed in the 1940s but the "To Lynch a Negro Tonight" story was torn out, leaving many to speculate about what happened.[45]

In either case, crowds of white men began gathering between 6:00 and 7:00 p.m. at the courthouse. By 9:00 p.m., more than four hundred angry white men had arrived.[46] Tulsa County sheriff Willard M. "Bill" McCullough was tasked with keeping Rowland safe and in police custody at the courthouse. McCullough attempted to disperse the crowd by telling them that there would be no lynching.

With the lynching of Belton still fresh in the minds of the Black community, a group of armed men, between twenty-five and thirty total, went to the courthouse too and offered to help McCullough defend Rowland. Once the Black men arrived at the courthouse, McCullough attempted again to disperse the crowd by saying:

> "No one is going to be lynched here. There is not going to be a charge against the young man. The white girl has admitted that he did not harm her. She said she was nervous and scared, and so she screamed when he grabbed her. That is all there is to the case. She is a very nervous person, but she is not going to press charges because no harm was done. So, go home now. I give you my word the Negro will be released in the morning."[47]

---

[45] Chakraborty, "The massacre of Tulsa's 'Black Wall Street'."

[46] Ellsworth, *Death in a Promised Land*, 49.

[47] Hirsch, *Riot and Remembrance*, 86.

For obvious reasons, the Black men who came to protect Rowland objected. If the police weren't going to press charges, why was he arrested in the first place? However, the small group of men left the courthouse. The white crowd did not and their numbers continued to grow. By approximately 10:30 p.m., the mob grew to two thousand people. As rumors of a growing crowd and lynching swept across the city, Greenwood responded by sending fifty to seventy-five men back to the courthouse to ensure the safety of Dick Rowland. They were urged by McCullough again to leave, as he stated that violence was easy to start but difficult to stop. As the Black men prepared to leave, E. S. MacQueen, a man who ran a failed bid to win the job as sheriff, attempted to disarm a Black man; many believe that this man was WWI veteran Johnny Cole. Why did MacQueen attempt to disarm him? Some theories point to MacQueen attempting to prove himself, to show voters that he should have been elected as sheriff rather than McCullough, who was attempting to disperse the crowds.

In 2005, a man by the name of Robert Fairchild recalled the interaction between Cole and MacQueen.[48]

> MacQueen: "Nigger, what are you going to do with that pistol?"
>
> Cole: "I am going to use it if I need to."
>
> MacQueen: "No, you give it to me."
>
> Cole: "Like hell I will."

A scuffle broke out between the two men. One shot was fired. For a moment, everyone was silent. Then the killing began.

---

[48] NPR, "1921 Riot Reveals Tulsa's History of Race Relations."

CHAPTER 3:

ASHES

Within an instant, the fate of Greenwood would be forever changed. After the first shot rang out, with no one being hit, bedlam ensued. At the courthouse, Black men were quickly getting killed and were outnumbered by more than 26-1. Many fled the courthouse to head back to the Greenwood district and the white mob gave chase. During the chaos, there were many accounts of the mob preventing emergency services from coming to the aid of Black people. In one instance, a group of white men prevented and threatened an ambulance from helping a Black man who was wounded by claiming that he was a "nigger" and "hunting for trouble."

Despite having an already sizable numbers advantage, white rioters did not simply stand their ground at the courthouse or defend what they felt was their city. They drove into Greenwood with the intent of crippling the Black economy and destroying Black bodies. En route to this aim, whites looted for guns and ammunition. One often-cited store was J.W. Mcgee's Sporting Goods, located on Second Street, where approximately $43,000 worth of property was taken, including jewelry.[49]

---

[49] Hirsch, *Riot and Remembrance,* 91.

As this was happening, the Tulsa Police Department took a different strategy. In previous instances with white mobs, the police department put forth some albeit minimal effort to prevent violence from occurring. That would not be the case this time. Tulsa's Police Department actually deputized the mob, many of whom were at the courthouse just moments earlier attempting to lynch Dick Rowland. The lynch mob in Tulsa went from a fringe group of people, one that operated in ways that the true authorities could not, to becoming legitimately "the authorities" themselves. At the county courthouse men were being sworn in as "Special Deputies" specifically to kill Black residents and protect white women.

> We are deputizing groups of men with automobiles to patrol the streets that separate the white and Negro sections of town. We want to be certain that a lot of black men don't sneak over and rape and kill a lot of white women during the night.[50]

One of those special deputies was Laurel G. Buck, a white bricklayer who was instructed to, "Get a gun, and get a nigger."[51] The notion that Black men were animals whose main goal was to rape white women was a common trope of the time and continues today.

*****

[50] Hirsch, *Riot and Remembrance*, 92.

[51] Oklahoma Commission to Study the Tulsa Race Riot of 1921, "Tulsa Race Riot," 193.

Wilmington, North Carolina 1898

In November 1898, white supremacists in Wilmington, North Carolina, overthrew the local government and destroyed the city's Black-owned newspaper while killing dozens (if not hundreds) in the process.[52] At the time, Wilmington was the state's largest city and had a sizeable Black population. During the preceding election cycle of 1896, Democrats, who then occupied the far-right side of the political spectrum, were soundly defeated by white farmers and Black Republicans. North Carolina Democrats devised an all-too-familiar strategy of igniting white fear and anger.

The Democratic Handbook of 1898 states the following:

> It is useless for your leaders to tell the people of Greenville that there is no danger of negro domination, for it is there already . . . It is useless to tell the people of Wilmington that there is no danger of negro domination, when they see the negro policemen every day parading the streets in uniform and swinging the "billy," ready to let it fall upon the head of white and black alike.
>
> It is useless to tell the people of Newbern and the people of Craven County that there is no danger of negro rule, when they have seen a negro magistrate issue his warrant for the arrest of a white woman, put it in the hands of a negro constable, have her arrested and brought before him, and then when her attorneys asked to have her case sent for trial before some other Justice of the Peace, sent it before another

[52] Chakraborty, "When White Supremacists Overthrew a Government."

> negro magistrate, with a negro lawyer there to prosecute her. All this they have seen, and may see again any day.
>
> . . . This party turned the counties and towns of the east over to the negroes when it was in power before, and it is doing it again.
>
> The remedy for the danger is a restoration of the Democratic Party to power; for while it will do absolute justice to the negro, it will not make a ruler out of him. [53]

Their primary fears were Good Negro Government, also known as Negro Rule, and Black men threatening white womanhood. These fears were further bolstered by newspapers, as seen with *The Tulsa Tribune* and *Tulsa World*. Wilmington had *The News and Observer*, one of North Carolina's largest outlets for the Democratic Party. One Wilmington paper printed a speech to the Georgia Agricultural Society by Rebecca Felton, where she stated in August 1897: ". . . if it takes lynching to protect women's dearest possession from drunken, ravening human beasts, then I say lynch a thousand a week."[54] Rebecca Felton went on to become the first female senator in the US Congress and was the last slave owner to serve in the legislature in 1922.

Alexander Manly, the owner of the Black-owned *Daily Record*, responded to Felton, calling her a "so-called Christian", and continued by detailing the ways in which white men routinely preyed on Black women during slavery. He went on to say that

[53] State Democratic Executive Committee, "The Democratic Handbook, 1898," 40.

[54] US House of Representatives, "Felton, Rebecca Latimer."

Black men "were sufficiently attractive for white girls of culture and refinement to fall in love with them as is well known to all."[55]

But Manly did not stop there. "Teach your men purity," he continued. "Let virtue be something more than an excuse for them to intimidate and torture a helpless people. Tell your men that it is no worse for a black man to be intimate with a white woman, than for a white man to be intimate with a colored woman. You set yourselves down as a lot of carping hypocrites."

That column was used to further stoke white anger and was reprinted and shared in multiple newspapers in the region. This, along with overt voter intimidation against Black people, helped the Democrats win every seat that was up for election in 1898 but it didn't take away the financial standing of African Americans in Wilmington or the progress that had already been made.

The day after the election the White Declaration of Independence was unveiled by the Democrats. In essence, white men have had three separate declarations of independence since arriving on the continent. Jefferson's in 1776, the Ordinance of Secession in 1861 as a part of the US Civil War, and this declaration in Wilmington, a declaration which, at the time, had nothing to do with white people being denied opportunities or oppressed in any way. It was simply Black people having their own agency that fueled this sort of response. When Thomas Jefferson created the Declaration of Independence in 1776, he owned slaves, despite having the words "all men are created equal" etched in the parchment. In Wilmington and Tulsa, Black people were enjoying their unalienable rights of life, liberty, and the pursuit of happiness far too much in the eyes of white people.

[55] UNC Libraries, "A Horrid Slander."

This White Declaration covered seven main points, including shutting down Alexander Manly's paper, having him expelled from the town, and obstructing Black people from voting or obtaining jobs.

Below are a few excerpts from the declaration:

> We, the undersigned citizens of the City of Wilmington and County of New Hanover, do hereby declare that we will no longer be ruled, and will never again be ruled by men of African origin . . .
>
> We propose in future to give to white men a large part of the employment heretofore given to negroes because we realize that white families cannot thrive here unless there are more opportunities for the employment of the different members of said families.
>
> A climax was reached when the negro paper of this city published an article so vile and slanderous that it would in most communities have resulted in the lynching of the editor. We deprecate lynching and yet there is no punishment, provided by the courts, adequate for this offense. We therefore owe it to the people of this community and of this city, as a protection against such license in the future, that the paper known as the "Record" cease to be published and that its editor be banished from this community. [56]

A group of white men burned down *The Daily Record* building the next day. The more than two hundred armed men then marched to

[56] East Carolina University, "White Declaration of Independence."

City Hall and forced Republicans to resign, including the mayor of Wilmington. The mob then grew to about two thousand men and began killing Black people in the streets, their bodies eventually dumped in the river. The original estimates were that forty to sixty people were killed but experts now believe that the number of Black fatalities was much higher. The city of Wilmington would never regain its Black majority and the white supremacist group led by Alfred Waddell—now Mayor Waddell— implemented a poll tax, among other Jim Crow laws, that ensured Black people would never exercise political and economic power. Manly fled Wilmington, making his way to Washington, DC, by 1900, and later Philadelphia. He died in 1944.[57]

History books made poor efforts to accurately tell the story. There were also multiple reports of Wilmington residents who were turned away at libraries for seeking information about what happened, according to a 2019 Vox Media report. One 1949 North Carolina textbook simply summarized the massacre in Wilmington like so: "A number of blacks were jailed for starting a riot and a new white administration took over Wilmington's government."[58] An American domestic coup d'état was reduced to just Black people rioting, with a new administration simply gaining power.

Today many of Wilmington's schools and parks are named after the men who instigated the attack. And like Tulsa in 2001, North Carolina's General Assembly established a commission in 2000 to uncover the history of that tragic event. By May 31, 2006, the

[57] Umfleet, "Alex Manly."

[58] Ellis, "Pulitzer-Winning Journalist Tells Historically Untold Story of Wilmington Coup."

five-hundred-page *1898 Wilmington Race Riot Report* was released, eighty-five years to the day after the Tulsa Massacre.[59]

In 2016, Paul LePage, governor of Maine, used the same sexualized trope of Black and brown men being attracted to white women. In a botched attempt to combat the spread of drug related crime, LePage was quoted as saying, "the enemy right now . . . are people of color or people of Hispanic origin." He then went on to say, "They come up here, sell heroin, then they go back home. Incidentally, half the time they impregnate a young, white girl before they leave."[60]

LePage ignored the FBI's statistics showing 1,212 people were arrested on charges of drug sales or manufacturing in Maine in 2014. Of those, only 170 were Black, making up about 14 percent of the group, and almost all the rest were white.[61]

*****

Walter White, a man who passed for white with his light skin and blue eyes as a journalist for the NAACP, was one of the more than five hundred men who were deputized during the Tulsa massacre. "You can now go out and shoot any nigger and the law'll be behind you," Walter was told.[62]

The violence only escalated through the night. Greenwood was facing an angry white mob on the ground killing and looting,

---

[59] Umfleet, "1898 Wilmington Race Riot Report."

[60] Phillips, "LePage Doubles Down: 'The Enemy Right Now' is 'People of Color'."

[61] BBC News, "Maine Governor Paul LePage Criticized for 'Racist' Remarks."

[62] Hirsch, *Riot and Remembrance*, 93.

with "deputies" accelerating the violence by preventing access to necessary medical care for those who were harmed.

And then came the attacks from the sky.

Tulsa, Oklahoma may very well be the first place where planes were used in an attack on American soil. Numerous reports circulated claiming that there were at least six planes used to bomb and gun down residents in the Greenwood District. Officials, however, claimed that the planes were only used to communicate with those on the ground. White, the NAACP journalist, wrote, "Eight aeroplanes were employed to spy on the movements of Negroes and according to some were used in bombing the colored section."[63] According to writer and teacher Mary E. Parrish Jones, "more than a dozen aeroplanes went up and began to drop turpentine balls upon the Negro residences," but Mrs. Parrish did not give a source and it did not appear that she witnessed these acts herself, according to the original 2001 massacre report.[64] Not all historians agree, as bombing from the sky would have been inefficient, likely killing allies as well. There were several reports of burning but none of actual explosions. Other reports said men with guns were shooting from the planes. This also would have been difficult but not impossible. Finally, many accounts taken from those who survived noted that men with rifles were shooting from the hills. This could explain why there's been confusion around how the planes were used. Nonetheless, we do know planes were flown during the attack.

---

[63] Oklahoma Commission to Study the Tulsa Race Riot of 1921, "Tulsa Race Riot," 105.

[64] Ibid.

Greenwood would continue to burn throughout the night and into the next day. National Guard troops from Oklahoma City got to Tulsa around 9:15 a.m. on June 1, 1921. Around 11:30 a.m., martial law was declared throughout the city.[65] While the initial count was distorted, white newspapers only counted the number of white people who were killed. The official estimate, however, is around three hundred total deaths, with the great majority being Black. It was Walter White who initially put the death toll at 250. In his assessment, he cites O. T. Johnson, a Salvation Army major, who said that forty-seven men had been hired to bury 150 bodies in Oaklawn Cemetery.[66] Eunice Cloman Jackson, the wife of a Black mortician, claimed fifty years later that her stepfather helped dig fifty graves in Oaklawn Cemetery.[67]

It wasn't until July 2020 that the City of Tulsa began looking for possible mass grave sites. In 2019, scientists found a pit at Oaklawn Cemetery measuring 30 feet x 25 feet, large enough to fit up to one hundred bodies.[68] The Oklahoma Archaeological Survey identified four total areas where mass graves may exist.

After Greenwood was reduced to ash, Tulsa made quick moves to prevent Black Wall Street from ever rebuilding.

---

[65] Ellsworth, *Death in a Promised Land*, 61.

[66] Fenwick, "The Massacre That Destroyed Tulsa's 'Black Wall Street'."

[67] Oklahoma Commission to Study the Tulsa Race Riot of 1921, "Tulsa Race Riot."

[68] Booker, "Excavation Begins for Possible Mass Grave From 1921 Tulsa Race Massacre."

CHAPTER 4:

MAYBE IT AIN'T DONE BURNING YET

While hundreds of bodies were poured into what are still unmarked and unfound graves, what was once one of the wealthiest Black communities in the United States looked like a war zone. Everything that was built had been destroyed in just twenty-four hours. The entire thirty-five square block Greenwood District was burned off the map.

5 hotels.
31 restaurants.
8 doctors' offices.
2 movie theaters.
4 drug stores.
24 grocery stores.
1000+ homes.

Reduced to ash.

300 Black people dead.

The spirit of white supremacy was not done with Black Wall Street. On June 2, within forty-eight hours of the attack, officials from the Tulsa Real Estate Exchange met with the Public Welfare Board with an idea: Relocate Greenwood's Black population and make the area into an industrial site. *The Tulsa Tribune* published an article on June 3 titled, "The Plan to Move Negroes into New District." Essentially, they believed that this area would serve as an additional buffer to separate the Black population from the white population while economically benefitting whites. Tulsa mayor T.D. Evans said, "We should immediately get in touch with all the railroads with a view to establishing a Union Station on this ground. The location is ideal and all the railroads convenient."[69]

This has left some to speculate that the entire ordeal, from the Rowland-Page interaction to the attack, was essentially motivated by a desire to relocate Black people. After all, Page herself chose not to press charges.

As with most white supremacist movements throughout US history, the law was used to specifically target Black citizens. By June 7, the Tulsa City Council voted 4-0 to pass fire ordinance No. 2156 to include the Greenwood District. This move now made Greenwood a part of the official fire limits of the city of Tulsa, effectively preventing Black Wall Street from rebuilding. This move was encouraged by the Tulsa Real Estate Exchange and required that any newly constructed buildings be built with fire-resistant materials. This was yet another falsely color-blind tactic still employed today. On its surface, this act would seem logical and fair when you ignore the situational context of what happened one week prior. In addition, the new fire code requirements effectively priced-out Black businesses, and white people knew this.

[69] Ellsworth, *Death in a Promised Land*, 85.

When the *Tulsa Tribune* described the fire code and the interest of the Real Estate Exchange, they said that there "will never again be a negro quarter . . . This was accomplished this morning when the city commission passed an ordinance extending the fire limits to include this section, including the negro business section on Greenwood Avenue. Because of the building requirements laid on the district it is believed impossible that the negroes will again build there."[70]

The burning of Black Wall Street also served as a recruitment tool for the Ku Klux Klan. Pictures and postcards of burned-out buildings helped Tulsa's KKK chapter become one of the largest in the nation.[71] They used those postcards as a marketing tool to sell white supremacy and celebrate their power. It was a way to remind Black people what they were willing to do to showcase that power and served as a trophy for white people. By 1924, Tulsa was one of the few places that had a "junior" Ku Klux Klan for boys aged twelve to eighteen.[72]

In the immediate days after the massacre, close to four thousand Black people, nearly 40 percent of the entire Black population in Tulsa at the time, were gathered and put into internment camps at the Tulsa fairgrounds. Initially Black people were held from June 2 through June 7 and were only released if a white person could vouch for them. It was during this period that orders were issued that prevented Black people from owning guns. The city also

[70] Krehbiel, *Tulsa 1921*, 142.

[71] Oklahoma Commission to Study the Tulsa Race Riot of 1921, "Tulsa Race Riot," 11.

[72] Ellsworth, *Death in a Promised Land*, 22.

passed an order preventing funerals to be held in churches. The city claimed the churches were used as shelters, even though only white churches were in fact being used as shelters and most of the dead were Black. Had funerals been held for the African Americans who were murdered, they certainly wouldn't have been held in white churches.

Field Order No. 4 instituted forced labor:

> All the able bodied negro men remaining in detention camp at the fairground and other places in the city of Tulsa will be required to render such service and perform such labor as required by the military Commission . . . able bodied women, not having the care of children, will also be required to perform such service as may be required in the feeding and care of refugees.[73]

As the laws of the city were changing, so too was a narrative around what happened and who was to blame. Almost immediately, media outlets and leaders began shifting the blame, citing that Black people alone caused the "riots." Many blamed what they saw as Black people's new inflated views of equal rights after experiencing a world beyond Jim Crow. This coincided with the "New Negro" movement at the time, partially fueled by W.E.B. Du Bois and Black WWI veterans returning home. African Americans were moving away from the accommodationist philosophy of Booker T. Washington. They felt that the Atlanta Compromise of 1895 was a

---

[73] Ellsworth, *Death in a Promised Land*, 75.

failed endeavor after witnessing what happened in Wilmington just three years later, the Atlanta Riots in 1906, and the Red Summer of 1919.

Washington attempted to find a middle ground in which whites would not be bothered with cries for equal treatment and voting rights in exchange for allowing Black people to work and establish their own economic systems and vocational training. He felt that respect with whites was something to be gained through economic merit, that if your race were "useful" then white people would not disrespect or abuse it.

> "No race that has anything to contribute to the markets of the world is long in any degree ostracized. It is important and right that all privileges of the law be ours, but it is vastly more important that we be prepared for the exercise of these privileges."
>
> -Booker T. Washington, 1895 Atlanta, GA
> The Atlanta Compromise

He was wrong. The Greenwood District had done mostly everything Washington outlined in his compromise. After all, it was Washington himself who visited Tulsa and gave the area its nickname. Despite being one of the wealthiest Black communities in the nation, wealth and prosperity didn't buy respect or dignity from white people.

The "New Negro" knew this, understanding that white people operated from a place of fear. S.P. Freeling, Oklahoma's attorney general, spoke at Hotel Tulsa just three days after the massacre, saying, "The cause of this riot was not Tulsa. It might have happened anywhere for the Negro is not the same man he was thirty years ago when he was content to plod along his own road accepting the white man as his benefactor. But the years have passed, and the Negro has been educated and the race papers have spread the thought of racial equality. Then came the war and in the army the Negro learned the value of organization . . . And in this organization there lies a force that is liable to start trouble anytime."[74]

One of those "race papers" that Feeling referred to was W.E.B. Du Bois' *The Crisis,* which published his first issue in November 1910. Over the next decade, Du Bois published numerous thoughts on the state of Black people in the country. In May 1919, he wrote an editorial called "Returning Soldier" in *The Crisis:*

> A dominant minority does not want Negroes educated. It wants servants, dogs, whores and monkeys. And when this land allows a reactionary group by its stolen political power to force as many black folk into these categories as it possibly can, it cries in contemptible hypocrisy . . .
>
> It organizes industry to cheat us. It cheats us out of our land; it cheats us out of our labor. It confiscates our savings. It reduces our wages. It raises our rent. It steals our profit. It taxes us without representation. It keeps us consistently and universally poor, and then feeds us on charity and derides our poverty . . . This is the country to which we Soldiers of Democracy return.

[74] Hirsch, *Riot and Remembrance*, 127.

> We do not marshal every ounce of our brain and brawn to fight a sterner, longer, more unbending battle against the forces of hell in our own land.
>
> *We return.*
> *We return from fighting.*
> *We return fighting.*[75]

It was with articles like this that some in Tulsa blamed W.E.B. Du Bois for the massacre since he came to Greenwood in April 1921 a month before the attack. Du Bois was, "The most vicious negro man in America, he had something to do with the riot," said Bishop E.D. Mouzon to his congregation the Sunday following the massacre.[76] Blame for the massacre would be discussed in the months and years that followed. Officially, the Negro was blamed for starting the riot, according to a report issued by a grand jury on June 25. In summary, the report stated that the white crowd gathered at the courthouse for curiosity and that there was no "mob spirit" among the white crowd, no talk of lynching, no guns. It stated that the whites who gathered at the courthouse were quiet until "the arrival of armed negroes" suddenly caused the riot. The grand jury also found "agitation among the negroes for social equality" as an indirect secondary cause.[77]

After the fire codes were passed, there was an immediate defense mounted by B.C. Franklin, Isaac Spears, and P.A. Chappelle with the

[75] DuBois, "Returning Soldiers."

[76] Krehbiel, *Tulsa 1921,* 122.

[77] Oklahoma Commission to Study the Tulsa Race Riot of 1921, "Tulsa Race Riot," 89.

help of a white attorney from Alabama named Mather Eakes. They challenged the fire code on behalf of Black property owners who were pressured to sell their land to white developers. They presented their case in front of a three-judge panel. On the morning of June 7, Judge W.B. Williams announced that the ordinance was illegal in a unanimous decision, giving Black residents an avenue to rebuild.[78] By September 1921, the charges against Dick Rowland were dropped. It was rumored that he moved to the Pacific Northwest, where he died sometime in the 1950s.[79] There are no records indicating what happened to Sarah Page after the night of June 1.

*****

For many native Tulsans like myself, this is where the story ends. Black Wall Street amassed incredible wealth, Dick Rowland tripped and bumped into Sarah Page, and a white mob burned down one of the most self-sustaining Black communities in the United States. The end.

If you learned anything about the Tulsa Race Massacre growing up here, those three lines are about as detailed as the history lesson got. This, however, was not the end of the story.

It is often the case that the "winners" write the history books. In the case of Tulsa, OK, winners are also able to erase and omit history from the books altogether. Many of those who grew up in Tulsa in the decades after the Tulsa Race Massacre had no idea that the event even occurred and usually didn't find out about this injustice until

78 Krehbiel, *Tulsa 1921*, 196.

79 Krehbiel, "Tulsa Race Massacre: What Happened to Sarah Page."

they left the city and attended college. This included former Tulsa mayor Bill LaFortune, who didn't know of the massacre.[80] The civil rights attorney for the 2016 murder of Terence Crutcher, Demario Solomon-Simmons, didn't know about the massacre either. "No, I'm from Tulsa. That's not accurate," Demario recalled telling his African American history professor who'd brought up the massacre at the University of Oklahoma in 1998. "I went to school on Greenwood. I've never heard of this ever."[81]

These stories were not at all uncommon. There were no memorials to honor the dead until seventy-five years after the massacre in 1996. History textbooks from the 1920s and '30s failed to mention what happened to the Greenwood District. This was not an innocent case of overlooking something; it was a deliberate cover-up. Not only was the article that sparked the massacre removed from *The Tulsa Tribune*'s archives but scholars found years later the police and state documents associated with the event were also missing. Pulitzer Prize-winning author Daniel J. Boorstin grew up in Tulsa and was six years old during the massacre. Despite writing a book titled *Hidden History*, along with twenty other books, and becoming the librarian of Congress in 1975, he barely mentioned Black Wall Street. This is even more disturbing because his father Sam Boorstin was the attorney for *The Tulsa Tribune* and could have been a primary source of information.[82] Boorstin wrote this about Tulsa in 1994: "Dark shadows such as the relentless segregation, the brutal race riots of

---

[80] Tresniowski, "Burned Into Memory."

[81] McDonnell, "Watch '60 Minutes' Delves Into the Haunting History of the 1921 Tulsa Race Massacre!"

[82] Hirsch, *Riot and Remembrance*, 196.

the 1920s and the Klu Klux Klan. But these were not visible or prominent in my life."[83]

Ultimately it was the Black teachers, those who were the descendants of the survivors, who ensured that their students knew. State Representative Don Ross, who helped authorize the commission to study the massacre in 1997, learned about it from W.D. Williams, a survivor of the massacre at age 15. Williams was a history teacher at Booker T. Washington High School; Williams's parents owned the Dreamland Theater and other businesses in the Greenwood District.[84] Upon learning this information, Ross, his student, just like Solomon-Simmons decades later, lashed out. "Greenwood was never burned. Ain't no 300 people dead. We're too old for fairy tales," Ross said to Williams.[85] The next day Ross was asked to stay after class. "What do you think of that, fat mouth?" Williams asked as he showed Ross the postcards of Greenwood on fire.

Other than Mary Elizabeth Jones Parrish's *Race Riot 1921: Events of the Tulsa Disaster*, there had not been much research completed on the topic. In fact, less than twenty-four copies of Parrish's book were originally published. It was reprinted after hitting the public domain in the 1990s. Parrish was the only eyewitness survivor of the massacre who was a trained journalist.[86] Decades later, in 1982, Dr. Scott Ellsworth, a native of Tulsa, wrote *Death in a Promised Land*. This was the same year that Don Ross was elected to his

[83] Ibid.

[84] Oklahoma Commission to Study the Tulsa Race Riot of 1921, "Tulsa Race Riot," iv.

[85] Ibid., v.

[86] Gates, "Reprinting of 'Race Riot, 1921' Filling Gaps in Tulsa's History."

first term in the Oklahoma House of Representatives. Ellsworth's book was considered one of the first full accounts of the massacre, including the historical context in the years prior to 1921 and what happened in the years after.

According to many, it was the April 1995 Oklahoma City bombing that brought residual attention to Tulsa and Black Wall Street. The Oklahoma Commission to Study the Tulsa Race Riot of 1921 highlighted this parallel. According to an overview written by John Hope Franklin and Scott Ellsworth, "The Murrah Building bombing is, without any question, one of the greatest tragedies of Oklahoma history. And well before the last memorial service was held for the last victim, thousands of Oklahomans made it clear that they wanted what happened on that dark day to be remembered."

A total of 168 people died, nineteen of whom were children, on April 19, 1995. As a native Oklahoman, I too will never forget. At the time, I was only five years old. Before I would witness the September 11th attacks in the sixth grade on live television, the OKC Bombing was the first time I recognized terrorism, completely oblivious that the very ground that I walked to school on, the streets that I took to get home, and the fields that I played football on were also sacred ground.

At the time, the OKC Bombing was billed as the worst attack on American soil since the Civil War. But as author Tim Madigan writes, "That dubious honor also belonged to Oklahoma, but to the city 100 miles east; it's just that television cameras weren't around in Tulsa on the morning of 1921 when whites came pouring in over the tracks . . . so instead of days of national mourning and the race to build a fitting monument, the world got out a big broom and swept the obliteration of Greenwood under a huge carpet." Black Tulsans carried the burden, the shame, the history, and the ashes of this painful past for more than seventy years before it received proper attention and care.

Between 1996, when construction of the Black Wall Street Memorial began, and 2002, new books began cropping up about the Tulsa Race Massacre, though it was still widely referred to as a riot. The first book I encountered as a child was Hannibal B. Johnson's *Black Wall Street: From Riot to Renaissance* in Tulsa's historic Greenwood District in 1998. I remember the book because of its distinct cover with colorful drawings of Black businesses and a rainbow in the background. My father would read us sections of the book from time to time. In 2001, the same year that the Oklahoma Commission report was released, *The Burning: Massacre, Destruction, and the Tulsa Race Riot of 1921* by Tim Madigan was published. One year later, James S. Hirsch would publish *Riot and Remembrance: America's Worst Race Riot and Its Legacy.*

Within just two years, the OKC Bombing Memorial began construction, which was included in Oklahoma history textbooks and field trips. It wasn't until February 2020 that the Oklahoma Department of Education included the massacre in the curriculum thanks in part to my father, Kevin Matthews Sr., who was elected to the Oklahoma State Senate. Prior to this, if the massacre was taught at all, it was at the discretion of individual teachers, many of whom omitted it altogether, assuming they knew of the event to begin with.

*****

If you're from Tulsa, you likely remember the very first time you heard about the Tulsa Race Massacre. After the denial phase, you also tend to remember the first few questions you asked after hearing about it: "Why didn't I learn about this?" "Why didn't they rebuild?" For years, I was taught to believe that June 1, 1921, was the end of the story and that the Black community didn't attempt to rebuild, that Black people gave up and left Oklahoma.

To a degree, this is true. One of the wealthiest Black men in Tulsa pre-massacre, J.B. Stradford, was wrongfully accused of starting the "riot." He eventually fled to Chicago to rebuild what he once had in Tulsa, never fully succeeding. Stradford reportedly lost $125,000, which at the time of this writing would be worth $1.6 million. This was nearly twice the amount lost by O.W. Gurley, the second wealthiest Black man in Tulsa. Gurley never recovered financially from the disaster either and ended up moving to California. Neither of these men, nor the thousands of other Black Tulsans, would be able to collect any insurance payments. This was due to a riot clause which exempted insurance companies from paying. Other citizens, like B. C. Franklin, stayed in Tulsa. His son, John Hope Franklin, went on to become one of the nation's top scholars in African American history, winning the Presidential Medal of Freedom in 1995.

One of the side effects of the massacre was a mass Black exodus from Tulsa. The Black population in Tulsa decreased by 71 percent, but those who stayed in the years after were committed to rebuilding.[87] By 1926, Tulsa had more hotels than Harlem and was a center for jazz and entertainment.

[87] Hirsch, *Riot and Remembrance*, 173.

Jessie O. Thomas was a Booker T. Washington protegee and social worker. In 1929, he went to Tulsa and stated: "There is probably no other case in the history of America where a group of people in similar hostile community so quickly and so completely rebuilt a 'new Jerusalem upon the ashes of a fallen city' with so limited financial resources."[88] At the time that Thomas came to Tulsa, the Greenwood District had twenty-five grocery stores, a life insurance company, restaurants, architects, and doctors.[89]

The Black economy in Tulsa was still very much based on entertainment-related businesses such as pool halls and jazz clubs. In addition to this, a large segment of Tulsa's Black population relied on domestic service work and brought that money back across the railroad tracks to Greenwood. When the Great Depression hit in August 1929, many of those domestic workers lost their jobs, thereby reducing the income that circulated through Black businesses. By 1936, three years after the end of the Depression, white lenders owned more than 30 percent of all the property in Greenwood. During World War II, Tulsa's economy picked up again as the US began producing but fell again when the war concluded. By 1978, only two Black-owned businesses remained.

"There are two ways which will destroy a black community. One is by building a freeway through it, the other is by changing the zoning laws," said Dr. John Hope Franklin.[90] In the 1960s, I-244 was built right through the Greenwood District. This tactic of running highways through Black communities began in the 1930s

[88] Ibid.

[89] Ibid.

[90] Ellsworth, *Death in a Promised Land.*

but accelerated in the '50s and '60s under the guise of "urban renewal." Celebrated author James Baldwin saw it differently. "Urban renewal means Negro removal" he said in an April 1963 interview with WNDT-TV in New York City.[91] In Detroit, Black neighborhoods like Paradise Valley and Black Bottom were dismantled after highway I-375 cut through the neighborhood. This also happened in Los Angeles, Nashville, Chicago, Pittsburgh, St. Louis, and dozens of other cities. In Atlanta, for example, Mayor Bill Hartsfield used a highway as "the boundary between the white and Negro communities."[92]

Whites in Tulsa never wanted the Black community to survive. This was well documented since Oklahoma reached statehood in 1907. It was also evident in the fire code and the subsequent news articles describing how it would be nearly impossible to rebuild.

Today, residents in Greenwood District and, by extension, north Tulsa still feel like there's a significant amount of people who don't want the Black community to survive. This is evidenced by a lack of access to fresh foods, healthcare, and banking, coupled with over-policing. Black Wall Street burned in 1921, but some Black Tulsans today will tell you, *"Maybe it ain't done burning yet."*

---

[91] CQ Researcher, "Urban Renewal Under Fire."

[92] Kruse, "What Does a Traffic Jam in Atlanta Have to Do With Segregation?"

CHAPTER 5:

TULSA TODAY

I often wonder how the legacy of the Tulsa Race Massacre affects the attitudes of Black Tulsans today and if it had an impact on how the Black community reacted to police brutality cases. Protests against police brutality became massive focal points and attracted weeks of national attention as social media platforms played an essential role in helping communities organize and call attention to certain issues. Notable cases included the death of Michael Brown in 2014 in Ferguson, MO, Eric Garner in New York, NY, also in 2014, Philando Castile in 2016, just outside of Minneapolis, MN, and George Floyd in 2020, also in Minneapolis. All were Black men unjustly killed by police officers, three on camera.

The protest over Floyd was one that the world had not seen before, with dozens of cities across the globe chanting his name in the streets for weeks. In England, protestors threw a statue of 17th century slave trader Edward Colston into Bristol Harbor. Tens of thousands gathered, from the Champs de Maris in Paris to the US embassies in Ireland, Kosovo, and South Africa. One reason for such a strong international reaction was the coronavirus pandemic.

Most people who saw the video didn't have the usual assortment of outlets to distract them from what they'd just seen. Sports were mostly canceled, school was out, and many shows and movies had seen their release dates pushed back as well. Floyd's death also stood out because it appeared to be in slow motion with people around, including other officers who could have saved his life. Another part of this dynamic is the fact that two men were killed in the same area within a few years of each other on video. This dynamic of two men on video being killed from the same city was exactly what happened in Tulsa in 2015 with Eric Harris and in 2016 with Terence Crutcher. Just like Minneapolis, if any city had the right to be upset and display anger, it would have been Tulsa. But that's not what happened. While protests and marches were held, they didn't garner the size or attention of later movements. Internally, I wondered if the legacy of the Tulsa Massacre still loomed so large, especially considering the response to protests that we've seen in Ferguson, Minneapolis, and Portland, that we were afraid to see a reenactment of the 1921 murders.

We now know that if those fears existed after Crutcher and Harris were killed, that any fear of an attack by police officers or white supremacist groups wasn't irrational. Minneapolis police issued a warrant for a man associated with the Aryan Cowboys, a white supremacist gang, for inciting the rioting in Minneapolis in July 2020.[93] The unidentified person, known at the time only as "Umbrella Man," was caught on video breaking windows at an AutoZone store. The mayor of Minneapolis, Jacob Frey, tweeted, "We are now confronting white supremacists, members of organized crime, out of state instigators, and possibly even foreign actors to destroy and destabilize our city and region."

[93] Sidner, "Minneapolis Police Identify 'Umbrella Man'."

As waves of protests swept across the country because of the deaths of George Floyd and Breonna Taylor, some cities responded by painting murals on the street. Most notably Washington, DC's Department of Public works painted "Black Lives Matter" in bright yellow on Sixteenth Street NW just north of Lafayette square, directly in front of the White House. On June 5, 2020, DC mayor Muriel Bowser renamed the area Black Lives Matter Plaza. This mural was a strong symbolic gesture to put the Black Lives Matter movement into the mainstream. Yet with this transition came conflict. Dozens of cities across the country emulated this action. One of those cities was Tulsa, OK, where those same words, Black Lives Matter, were painted in bright yellow, in all caps, on Greenwood Avenue in the center of Black Wall Street.

In Tulsa, the mural appeared on June 18, two days before President Trump would speak in the city and just seventeen days after the ninety-ninth anniversary of the massacre that occurred on that very street. While the city didn't officially sanction the mural like Washington, DC, the words "Black Lives Matter" on Black Wall Street and on Juneteenth isn't a controversial or political statement. Of all places, Black lives should certainly matter here, and no one who lives or works in Tulsa should have taken an exception to the message. When the mural appeared, and in the days shortly after, there were almost no complaints from Greenwood District residents. However, as the history of Tulsa and this country has shown, Black joy and empowerment have always been a threat to white supremacy and racism.

On Wednesday, July 29, the Tulsa City Council ordered that the mural be removed. This was due to a counter-group called Back the Blue, which made a request to paint a similar mural. Similar to the groups All Lives Matter and White Lives Matter, Back the Blue exists to dilute the problem of police brutality against African Americans and deflect attention away from racist actions and policies.

It has been well documented that the Black Lives Matter movement is explicitly against police brutality and is *not* anti-police. Many white Americans, rather than listen, employed willful ignorance. Through the years the strategy is simple: distract the message and rebrand it to seem anti-American and unpatriotic, then attempt to use the law to block, erase, or derail the overall movement.

This was the case in 2016 when San Francisco 49ers' quarterback Colin Kaepernick began kneeling during the National Anthem. Instead of listening to the words of US Army veteran Nate Boyer, who asked Kaepernick to kneel instead of sitting, many white Americans, including then-president Donald Trump, distorted the gesture into an anti-American, anti-military protest.

Teammate Eric Reid, who knelt with Kaepernick, stated in *The New York Times*:

> We chose to kneel because it's a respectful gesture. I remember thinking our posture was like a flag flown at half-mast to mark a tragedy . . . It baffles me that our protest is still being misconstrued as disrespectful to the country, flag and military personnel. We chose it because it's exactly the opposite. It has always been my understanding that the brave men and women who fought and died for our country did so to ensure that we could live in a fair and free society, which includes the right to speak out in protest.[94]

[94] Reid, "Eric Reid: Why Colin Kaepernick and I decided to Take a Knee."

Despite this form of peaceful protest being suggested by a member of the military, the same military that people were insisting that Kaepernick disrespected, the entire narrative was diluted. President Trump, while in Alabama in 2017, suggested that those who didn't stand for the anthem shouldn't be in the country. He called it a "total disrespect of our heritage."[95] He didn't note that this "heritage" was soaked in anti-Black racism. The "Star Spangled Banner" clearly acknowledges this in the third verse:

"No refuge could save the hireling and the slave. From the terror of light or the gloom of the grave: and the star-spangled banner in triumph doth wave, O'er the land of the free and home of the brave."

Like the national anthem itself, the history about the oppression and killing of Black people in Tulsa was a footnote, something buried away and left unnoticed for decades.

The largest factor in the city council's decision was that essentially if you allow one message to be painted on the street then you have to allow all messages to be painted as well. So "Back the Blue" as well as "Babies' Lives Matter" must also be allowed; therefore the Black Lives Matter mural needed to be removed, with no one getting a mural. On the day the mural was scheduled to be erased, city officials found cardboard tombstones with the names of the victims of police brutality and the names of victims from the 1921 Tulsa Race Massacre at the intersection of Greenwood Avenue and Archer Street. As a result, the city offered a temporary hold on the removal to work out and discuss actions.

---

[95] Associated Press, "NFL Anthem Dispute."

On August 9, residents woke up to find the 250-foot mural vandalized with a blue line of paint splattered across the text, most likely signifying the "thin blue line," a term popular in the pro-police community that asserts police are the line that prevents society from falling into disorder and violence. It is also commonly displayed as a black and white American flag with one blue line.

This action was overtly racist, but it also points out the hypocrisy and the common historical irony that white supremacy continues to put itself in. The very group that claims to support police, rather than create their own mural in front of a police station, decided to deface and cross out a mural celebrating Black life. It boils down to this: The very group that so staunchly supports law enforcement felt so strongly about devaluing Black life that they were willing to break the law to state their case. It also dismantles the argument that the Blue Lives Matter/Back the Blue crowd is about supporting law enforcement. Blue Lives Matter exists explicitly to dilute, distract, and destroy the idea of Black Lives Matter while operating under the façade of patriotism and law and order. The same people who choose to fly the Confederate flag have flown the thin blue line as well, a dynamic on display at the neo-Nazi rally in Charlottesville, VA, in 2017.

By themselves and out of context, you may be led to the belief that blue line symbols aren't racist. However, context is always important, and one must always ask when did the symbols gain popularity? Where are these symbols used the most? Who's promoting these symbols and what are their commonly held beliefs? Using this common framework, it's easy to spot which symbols are created for general support or affinity and which ones represent oppression and racism.

The Confederate battle flag, as well as Confederate monuments, serve as a good starting point. The Confederate battle flag wasn't widely displayed until the 1950s and '60s. It took nearly one hundred years after the Civil War for the flag to become popular at KKK rallies, lynchings, or the integration of a neighborhood or school. It wasn't until 1962 when South Carolina started flying the Confederate flag at the state Capitol. At the time, South Carolina claimed that they were celebrating the hundredth anniversary of the Civil War. It wasn't until 2015, after a white supremacist killed nine Black church members, that the flag was finally removed. In 1956, the state of Georgia redesigned their state flag to include the Confederate battle flag. Georgia redesigned their state flag in 2001 but still included a small image of the 1956 flag at the bottom. It wouldn't be until 2003 that Georgia updated its flag to the one that is known today, sans Confederate symbolism. Mississippi had the Confederate flag niched in the left corner of its state flag until the summer of 2020.

During the summer of 2020, NASCAR banned the display of Confederate flags as well. The organization's only Black driver, Bubba Wallace, began racing with a #BlackLivesMatter car with the words "Compassion, Love, Understanding." Just a few days later, a "Thin Blue Line" vehicle was driven by Mike Harmon with the words "Back the Blue" painted on the side of the car. It's no coincidence the moment NASCAR's only Black driver is highlighted, and the Confederate flag taken down, that a Thin Blue Line car was announced as a reaction. Harmon had the opportunity to have a pro-police car previously but chose to make this statement at the height of the Black Lives Matter movement in response to the cancellation of a white supremacist symbol.

The Thin Blue Line flag did not gain traction until 2014, the year that protests sprang up across the country due to the unarmed killings of Eric Garner, Michael Brown, and Tamir Rice. The creator of the thin blue line American flag's and founder of Thin Blue USA Andrew Jacob explained the flags meaning to *The Detroit News* in 2017: "The black above represents citizens and the black below represents criminals."[96] It's important to note how this type of symbolism is dangerous, closely connecting to racism in America. Criminals, whether nonviolent or not, are still citizens and should be treated as such with due process under the law. In the context of African Americans, one of the reasons that slavery and racism have persisted for so long is because Black people weren't seen as humans, that our Black skin was a dividing line between human and animal. To be exact, Black people were considered to be only three-fifths of a person. This dates back to the Constitutional Convention in 1787, where northern and southern states came up with the Three-Fifths Compromise to balance power. Southern slaveholders wanted their "property" counted in the census population, thus tipping the legislative scale in their favor. Northern states didn't want this, and both sides settled on assigning the value of Black people as just three-fifths of a free white person.

While the creator of the blue line flag stated that it is not a symbol of racism and hate and is meant to honor the officers who've fallen in the line of duty, such sentiment doesn't negate how the flag has been adopted and used. It also doesn't negate the fact that a flag had already existed for police officers who've fallen. The flag's creation follows the same white supremacist tradition that has used

[96] Sharlet, "A Flag for Trump's America."

patriotism and supposedly racially neutral terms to satisfy the goals of white supremacy. The thin blue line flag uses regular American iconography, which doesn't immediately alienate most people like the Confederate flag or the swastika symbol, because it speaks to a sensibility that we find normal and unoffensive. The blue line flag was spotted during the US Capitol insurrection in January 2021. The irony here is that the group carrying the flag supposedly meant to support law enforcement ultimately killed an officer while breaking into the US Capitol in an attempt to overturn the 2020 presidential election results.

This tradition is essentially a dog whistle and has been executed in symbols, language, and policy. This was famously explained by republican strategist Lee Atwater in 1981:

> You start out in 1954 by saying, "Nigger, nigger, nigger." By 1968 you can't say "nigger"—that hurts you, backfires. So you say stuff like, uh, forced busing, states' rights, and all that stuff, and you're getting so abstract. Now, you're talking about cutting taxes, and all these things you're talking about are totally economic things and a byproduct of them is, blacks get hurt worse than whites . . . "We want to cut this," is much more abstract than even the busing thing, uh, and a hell of a lot more abstract than "Nigger, nigger."[97]

These symbols and policies have worked to continuously suppress the reconstruction of Black Wall Street today. For nearly two decades, the city of Tulsa refused to look for the mass graves after

[97] Perlstein, "Exclusive: Lee Atwater's Infamous 1981 Interview."

the initial 2001 report cited Oaklawn Cemetery and Newblock Park as potential areas for mass graves. It wasn't until 2019 that Mayor G. T. Bynum decided to begin the search. By October 2020, eleven coffins were found in Oaklawn Cemetery. As of this writing, it has not yet been determined that the remains are from the massacre.

*****

In 2019, Tulsa city published its annual Tulsa Equality Indicator study. It found that 17 percent of the population is Latino, 15 percent are Black, 6 percent are two or more races (which generally include Native American), 4 percent are Native American, and an additional 4 percent identified as Asian or another race. Despite nearly half of the city's population being made up of people of color, there was only one city council person who was nonwhite. Tulsa has never had a nonwhite mayor in its history, dating back to 1898. (While Oklahoma didn't become a state until 1907, Tulsa incorporated and elected its first mayor on January 18, 1898.)

The city launched the Tulsa Equality Indicators project in 2017, with the first study published in 2018. This was made possible with the help of the City University of New York (CUNY) and the Rockefeller Foundation. The study attempts to measure, track, and understand social progress and inequality in the city in six key areas, also known as themes: economic opportunity, education, housing, justice, public health, and services. (Services is defined as libraries and public transit.)

In the 2019 version of this study, it cites a list of "accomplishments" that the city has achieved in addressing historic racism. The list includes renaming schools and areas that were previously named after Confederate generals like Robert E. Lee, including renaming Brady Street. Brady Street and the Brady Theater were named after Wyatt Tate Brady, a politician and KKK member who was considered a "founder" of Tulsa. Brady, born in 1870, was also active in the Sons of the Confederate Veterans, an organization that the KKK regularly recruited from. It was also revealed that Brady was one of the major organizers behind the 1917 IWW attack, a major precursor to the tensions that existed in 1921. All seven of the IWW members identified Tate Brady as the man who tarred and feathered them.[98] Brady was also appointed to the Tulsa Real Estate Exchange, the same organization that attempted to take land from the Black community just hours after the massacre. He committed suicide four years after the massacre in 1925 over the accidental death of his son, John Davis Brady, who was attending law school at the University of Virginia.

Another one of the accomplishments that the 2019 Tulsa Equality Indicators states is the successful effort in changing the name from the "Tulsa Race Riot" to the "Tulsa Race Massacre." Until 2018, the vast majority of people referred to the event as the "Tulsa Race Riot." This included books and news articles on the topic, many of which I've referenced in the process of writing this book. The 2001 report done by the state of Oklahoma was known as the "1921 Race Riot Commission." The use of the word "riot" had been a point of contention in recent history and beyond.

Dr. Olivia J. Hooker was one of the last known survivors of the Tulsa Race Massacre; she was six years old at the time of the attack. She later became the first African American woman to enter the

[98] This Land, "The Essential Guide to Tate Brady."

U.S. Coast Guard in 1945. In 2007, she testified in front of the US House of Representatives Judiciary Committee. There, she stated: "I am a survivor of what is known as the Tulsa Race Riot of 1921, but what was really a massacre of the Greenwood neighborhood of Tulsa."[99]

Mary E. Jones Parrish, also a survivor, titled her book as the *Events of the Tulsa Disaster* in 1923. A.J. Smitherman in a poem describing the event called it, "The Tulsa Race Riot and Massacre."

"There may have been a riot in Tulsa, but there was a massacre in Greenwood," wrote Nehemiah D. Frank, the founder of *The Black Wall Street Times,* a news media company in February 2018. He and others were behind the efforts to change the name to what was then known as the 1921 Race *Riot* Centennial Commission to the 1921 Race *Massacre* Centennial Commission (emphasis mine). This commission was established to "leverage the rich history surrounding the 1921 Tulsa Race Massacre by facilitating actions, activities, and events that commemorate and educate all citizens."[100]

While the term "massacre" is now widely adopted, not everyone agrees with the switch in language. We know that branding the attack as a riot was used to deny insurance claims. And while the word "riot" may have had a different connotation nearly one hundred years ago, it does imply that the massacre was simply an outbreak of disorder and chaos rather than a show of force by those who had power against those who did not. White men had a 26-1

[99] Subcommittee on the Constitution, Civil Rights and Civil Liberties, "Tulsa-Greenwood Race Riot."

[100] 1921 Tulsa Race Massacre Centennial Commission.

advantage in number; white men flew planes; white men used the police force to further terrorize Black people. To some, though, the word massacre implies that Greenwood offered up no resistance (which was not true). Others found the word "massacre" to be "too inflammatory." Carol Mann, in a letter to the editor, wrote to the *Tulsa World* in 2019: "As an elderly white resident of the Tulsa area, I finally become offended."[101] She went on to suggest that if the "powers that be" wanted a name that was more repulsive to choose "genocide, annihilation or bloodbath." In her letter, she did not directly express why the word "massacre" offended her or why she felt that the word "riot" was more appropriate.

Overall, the city scored 41.74 out of a possible 100, which was a 1.7-point improvement from 2018. The economic opportunity portion of the indicator is divided into three categories: business development, employment, and income. The data reveals that the legacy of the massacre as well as racism still work to disadvantage Black people in Tulsa today and, truthfully, throughout the entire country. Indicator #3 within economic development is the geography and payday loans category. It is defined as the ratio of rates of banks to payday lending establishments per 1,000 in population in south Tulsa, which is mostly white, and north Tulsa, which is predominantly Black. There were eleven banks for every one payday lender in south Tulsa, versus only 1.5 banks for every payday lender in north Tulsa. The city also measured race and median household income. It was $51,744 for whites compared to $30,902 for Black.

These are significant factors that contribute to the racial wealth gap in Tulsa and beyond. We know from years of research that the

[101] Mann, "Letter to the Editor."

majority of wealth in this country has been passed on through real estate. Much like the descendants of Tate Brady and many oil families that moved to the Tulsa area early on, some still have a significant portion of their wealth intact; the massacre robbed Black families of that possibility. The combination of having your business and home burned, of not being allowed to collect insurance damages or reparations, leaves very little to repair and rebuild from. Many of those families never returned to Tulsa or had to start from zero. The compounding interest in a business or an investment lost over one hundred years ago doesn't repair itself. That gap will always remain until direct actions are taken to correct it.

Hannibal B. Johnson, author of *Black Wall Street: Riot to Renaissance in Tulsa's Historic Greenwood District*, described this in June 2020: "The event that was the massacre, is actually a great disruptor of the economic wellbeing of black folks and it also disrupts the transfer of wealth intergenerationally."[102] This can even be seen in the way that some businesses still operate in Tulsa. The *Tulsa World*, one of the white-owned newspapers that reported the massacre, was founded in 1905. It remained in the Lorton family until 2013, when it was sold to Warren Buffett's BH Media for an undisclosed amount. We do know, however, that Lee Enterprises in 2020 bought the *Tulsa World* along with *The Buffalo News* for $140 million. This is wealth that had been allowed to operate and generate money for a family for more than one hundred years, from 1905 to 2013. We also know that the paper was worth tens of millions of dollars, supporting thousands of jobs over the years.

---

[102] Berman, "Trump Will Hold a Rally in Tulsa."

The Black-owned *Tulsa Star*, founded in 1912, wasn't given the same opportunity. It was destroyed in the massacre, forcing its founder A.J. Smitherman to flee. Smitherman worked for various Black-owned newspapers in Buffalo, NY, until he founded the *Buffalo Star* (later renamed *Empire Star*) in 1932, continuing the paper until his death in 1961.[103] We'll never know what the *Tulsa Star* and Smitherman's contributions might have been if not cut short.

At the time of this writing, the Greenwood District and north Tulsa as a whole still don't have many of the businesses and services they once had, which not only reduces the quality of life for the majority of Black residents but also the capacity to circulate money through the Black community, fostering a more stable ecosystem. When combined with the fact that Black income is nearly $20,000 less than white income, coupled with the 2008 financial crisis and the coronavirus pandemic of 2020, it's clear why Black Wall Street hasn't rebuilt itself from the ashes as many would hope. To do that would require a multi-pronged effort from government and community leaders and individuals. Until that day arrives, true progress and revival will wait.

[103] The Gateway to Oklahoma History, "Tulsa Star."

CHAPTER 6:

REBUILDING BLACK WALL STREET

Over the years, there have been a number of campaigns with the goal of trying to "rebuild Black Wall Street." In January 2020, the Greenwood Chamber of Commerce announced that it would be looking to raise $10 million to build and refurbish areas of the Greenwood District, as well as start a business incubator. The chamber did receive a $500,000 grant from the National Parks Service and started a GoFundMe page with a $1,000,000 goal. As of the writing of this book, the GoFundMe campaign has only raised $35,200.[104]

In 2018, Dream Tulsa, an initiative funded by the George Kaiser Family Foundation, attempted to attract Black entrepreneurs and innovators from across the country to the city. The goal was to make Tulsa the number one destination for entrepreneurs of color. In 2018, *Forbes* named Tulsa the number one city in the nation for young entrepreneurs and number one for women entrepreneurs.[105]

To understand and attempt to rebuild Black Wall Street today,

---

[104] GoFundMe, "Rebuild Greenwood: The Original Black Wall Street."

[105] Andrews, "Here's How Oklahoma's Black Entrepreneurs are Rebuilding 'Black Wall Street'."

you first have to understand how it was built and the context and conditions that led to its success.

#1 Intention

J.B. Stradford and O.W. Gurley bought sections of the Greenwood District and purposely sold it only to African Americans. Those who lived in Greenwood had pride and purposely spent their money in their own community to the point that white business owners felt that Black residents intimidated people into not buying from them. Hannibal Johnson told *Forbes* that Greenwood was seen as a place to escape oppression in the Deep South. That it was born out of necessity. It wouldn't have existed had it not been for Jim Crow segregation and the inability of Black folks to participate to a substantial degree in a larger, white-dominated economy.[106]

This is an important fact to note. The Black economy and ecosystem at that time and other romanticized times in history did not simply appear out of nowhere. They were intentionally built by direct action (and, in some cases, indirect reaction) to white terrorism and segregation. In either case, to rebuild a Black Wall Street today, whether it be in Tulsa or anywhere else in the country, it must be done with the explicit intention of uplifting the Black economy and Black businesses.

#2 Environment

As with any movement, proximity is important even in the age of technology. The entire Black population in Tulsa lived in the

---

[106] Huddleston, "'Black Wall Street': The History of the Wealthy Black Community and the Massacre Perpetrated There."

Greenwood District. This is primarily the case today. Throughout history, proximity has been shown to generate wealth if there's a common purpose and focus, along with resources. Today one of the most common examples of this is Silicon Valley in California. Google, Apple, Facebook, Netflix, Tesla, and Cisco Systems are all concentrated in this area. This is not by accident. This region had the benefit of major universities like Stanford, San Jose State, and the University of California at Berkeley supplying them with innovative talent and cutting-edge research. Stanford alone produced Google, LinkedIn, Instagram, Pandora Radio, Snapchat, and YouTube between the years of 2000 and 2015.

The same could be said about music and entertainment, and even sports. When you have a high concentration of people who are interested and focused in one area, you have a much greater likelihood of producing consistent and exceptional results. Atlanta's and New York's hip-hop scenes and Texas's and Florida's football talent are two good examples.

Rebuilding Black Wall Street will require a region that's focused on the same goal and putting its resources behind that goal.

#3 Business Ownership

While real estate remains the largest vehicle for the transfer of wealth, business ownership has often been the vehicle to generate the highest overall amount of wealth. Approximately two out of every three millionaires own their own business, with about 21 percent of their wealth tied to that business. By no means is business ownership perfect or would every single person need to own a business to rebuild Black Wall Street. It's clear, however, that a high number of entrepreneurs is important and can help drive an ecosystem that lifts an entire community. This works because as the community pours their money into a local business owner, that business continues to grow and hire those in the community. As the business thrives, so too does its employees, who are then able to spend more in other Black-owned businesses. The cycle is a never-ending loop if done correctly.

This is another reason why Silicon Valley has exploded the way that it has over the past thirty to forty years. People in this area received funding to start businesses and those businesses grew massively, which spurred a race for the best employees. As these companies grew, they were able to pay more in salaries and attract more talent. Those employees went on to buy homes and cars, helping increase the tax revenue for local governments.

Nonetheless, this doesn't make Silicon Valley perfect, as this sudden increase in wealth did have negative side effects for those who already lived in the area and couldn't keep pace with the price inflation that came with the millions of higher paying jobs. Silicon Valley has also been known to have a major diversity problem.

*****

Rebuilding Black Wall Street will help to avoid some of these issues, but attempting to build an ecosystem with the same tenets that were used in 1921 will not be efficient for today's economy. Many who imagined the renaissance or revival of Black Wall Street think that dozens of mom and pop shops will do the trick. However, mom and pop shops, whether they be Black owned or not, have been under attack for decades. In business, the landscape of competition has drastically changed, and while most people will point to an

Amazon as the Grim Reaper of small businesses, one can argue that the first Wal-Mart and other large national retail stores were the first culprits. A significant portion of business ownership has moved to the online landscape. While this can be an advantage for an entrepreneur because startup costs are significantly less, it does make it harder for a region and community to rally support in the same way they could for a brick and mortar business. For example, in the 1920s an entrepreneur in Atlanta didn't have to directly compete or be compared to a business owner in Tulsa, Harlem, or Detroit. In an online space, the competition is more wide open, and while your money may still go to a Black-owned business, your purchases may not have the same impact on hiring and supporting those in the community that you live in.

Today, it's much easier to run a company from your computer but also hire people across the world. This wasn't the case one hundred years ago. If you needed a secretary, you would likely hire someone from your church. If you need a secretary today, you could simply hire a virtual assistant from literally anywhere on the globe. If you build an ecosystem and environment for small businesses and entrepreneurs, you have to pay attention to how supply chains work and ensure that you have the resources in a particular city. Those resources must also be Black owned to truly foster a Black Wall Street.

For a more modern take on what a Black Wall Street could look like, many may turn to Atlanta, Georgia. Atlanta is often ranked number one for the best place for Black-owned businesses. It is also one of the few major cities that feature multiple HBCUs within a small area: Morehouse, Spelman, and Clark Atlanta University. While it's a bit more spread out, the DC, Maryland, and Virginia area is also flanked by prominent HBCUs like Hampton and Howard universities. While these areas may provide somewhat of a template for what a modern-day Black Wall Street could be, they don't solve the issue of creating a new environment, one that could exist in your backyard and not in three to four cities across the South. Perspective is important when trying to create a Black Wall Street.

The Greenwood District was just a neighborhood, not an entire city. For comparison, Wall Street itself in New York City is confined to a very small area less than half a mile but still wields considerable power. To rebuild Black Wall Street, it's more important to have a small yet unified district rather than a sprawling area. Keeping the focus on building a strong community is much more feasible and repeatable then attempting to build an entire metroplex. For comparison, this could also look similar to Harlem, which is a neighborhood in New York City, not its own borough like Brooklyn or Queens. But due to Harlem's distinct culture and collectiveness, it's earned national and international attention.

Beyond having a goal-oriented community, much more will be needed to create Black Wall Street in a modern sense. There are two ways in which this could happen: The first is by individual means, which include saving, investing, and other tactics that you can employ on a personal level; the second is at a more systemic level, which would require political capital and organizing. Both are important.

Keep in mind that the current state of the Black economy is not due to a lack of motivation or simply bad financial habits. The root cause has been structural racism. That must be acknowledged with any conversation regarding the resurrection of Black Wall Street. In today's context, especially in the context of entrepreneurship and homeownership, capital will be needed, and the number of Black-owned banks has declined. As of 2019, there were only twenty-one Black banks in the United States (forty-two when you include credit unions).[107] This is down from the forty-eight Black banks that existed in 2001 according to *The Washington Post*.[108]

The dwindling number of Black-owned banks increases the likelihood of financial discrimination in a number of different areas, which can work to devalue Black homes as well as deny access to loans to start a business. Borrowers with Black-sounding names were treated differently by lenders. In his book *The Black Tax: The Cost of Being Black in America,* Shawn D. Rochester states: ". . . the difference in the treatment between the applicants with white-sounding names and Black-sounding names had the same impact as if the applicant with Black-sounding names had a FICO credit score that was 71 points lower."[109] That variance alone is not only enough to have a loan declined but it can also result in significantly higher costs if that loan were approved.

In 2012, the Economic Policy Institute found that African American consumers with a 660 credit score were three times as likely to end up with higher-rate mortgages. Just over 21.4 percent of Black borrowers received higher-rate mortgages than white borrowers at just 6.2 percent despite having the exact same 660 FICO credit score. On the business side of things, Black-owned

---

[107] Williams, "Black-Owned Banks by State."

[108] Fletcher, "The Country's Last Black-Owned Banks are in a Fight for Their Survival."

[109] Rochester, *The Black Tax*, 17.

small businesses receive less than 2 percent of all money distributed through the Small Business Administration.[110] And only 1 percent of venture capital money goes to Black entrepreneurs.[111]

To further emphasize the reasons for the gap in wealth and opportunity between Black people and white people, look no further than the Homestead Act in 1862. This law distributed 246 million acres of land across the next sixty years to 1.5 million families. That land would be worth somewhere between $740 billion and $1.6 trillion as of 2015.[112] But out of those 1.5 million families that received land through the act, 99.73 percent went to white families. Researchers estimate that up to 93 million Americans today are direct beneficiaries of that program. Government action is a direct result as to why white families have a net worth of ten times more than Black families.

The Homestead Act was not a simple once-in-a-lifetime government action. The United States has a long list of laws that work to explicitly help white people while ignoring or directly crippling Black people. In Tulsa, local government enforced the fire code and built a highway to permanently suppress the Greenwood District.

This was also seen with the GI Bill in 1944, when the federal government invested $95 billion with the purpose to create opportunities for soldiers returning from WWII. Less than 2 percent went to Black veterans in New York and northern New

---

[110] Rochester, *The Black Tax*, 37.

[111] Albergotti, "Black Start-Up Founders Say Venture Capitalist Are Racist."

[112] Souffrant, "The Black Tax: The Cost of Being Black in America With Shawn Rochester."

Jersey, and less than 100 of the 67,000 mortgages insured by the GI Bill supported homes purchased by non-whites.[113]

To squarely place the blame of the racial wealth gap on Black spending habits ignores how wealth in this country was built. In every imaginable metric, from income to investments, entrepreneurship to employment, white people have designed these systems to benefit themselves on the basis of race. There's no other reason as to why African Americans are paid less than whites at every education level.[114] Or the fact that among college graduates, Black people have faced an unemployment rate that's double their white peers'. The Economic Policy Institute found that 85 percent of Black people would need to obtain a bachelor's degree for Black people to reach the same employment as white people. Currently only 24 percent of Black people have bachelor's degrees, compared to 36 percent for white people.[115]

Potential Policy Fixes

Attempting to fix these disparities through government policy will always be difficult. However, the problems that we face today were created explicitly through government policy itself. To have the most effective remedy to the wealth gap and other issues will require political organization. For some, a political remedy only exists at the federal level, but state and local policies should also be considered.

---

[113] Matthews, "What is the Racial Wealth Gap and How Can we Fix It."
[114] Ibid.
[115] Ibid.

In Tulsa, the case was made for reparations for survivors. The commission put together by Representative Don Ross specified that the report may contain "specific recommendations regarding whether or not reparations can or should be made."[116] Contextually, during this time the case for reparations was being made in other states. A Florida commission made payments of up to $150,000 to 1923 survivors of the Rosewood Massacre, where a mob of white men burned the predominantly Black town to the ground, with at least eight people killed. (The actual death toll was likely much higher.) The law passed in 1994 and allowed the descendants of the Rosewood Massacre to go to college in state tuition-free, making it one of the first states to grant some form of reparations. Since the law was passed, 297 students have received Rosewood Scholarships.[117] In the 1980s, the US government paid Japanese American families who were put into internment camps during World War II. Land and money had also been given to some Native American tribes for the numerous attacks and theft during the Manifest Destiny era in the nineteenth century as the United States felt compelled to expand to the west. At the time, this "destiny" was used to justify the removal of Native American people.

In yet another strange twist of irony, the president's Fourth of July speech (which occurred on July 3) in 2020 mentioned Manifest Destiny, saying, "Americans are the people who pursued our Manifest Destiny across the ocean, into the uncharted wilderness, over the tallest mountains and into the skies and even into the stars."[118]

---

[116] Krehbiel, "Race Riot Reparations Questioned."

[117] Samuels, "After Reparations."

[118] Morris, "What is Manifest Destiny?"

It is worth noting again that this speech occurred at Mount Rushmore, which is on sacred land for the Sioux Nation. Land that was taken, land that even the US Supreme Court ruled unconstitutional. "We are the people who dreamed a spectacular dream . . . and who carved our heroes into the face of Mount Rushmore," President Trump said. The person who carved these "heroes" was Gutzon Borglum, an artist aligned with the Ku Klux Klan.

Mount Rushmore was not Borglum's first time carving the "heroes" into the side of a mountain. Borglum drew up the proposal for a Confederate monument to feature Robert E. Lee, Stonewall Jackson, Jefferson Davis, and J.E.B. Stewart into Stone Mountain outside of Atlanta, Georgia. It was Helen Plane, the founder of the Atlanta chapter of the Daughters of the Confederacy, who approached Borglum in 1915, the same year that the film *The Birth of a Nation* was released. Plane worked out a deal with an Atlanta theater in which the venue would donate its proceeds from *Birth of a Nation* to the Stone Mountain project.[119] She wrote a letter to Borglum saying: "I feel that it is due to the Ku Klux Klan which saved us from domination and carpetbag rule, then it might be immortalized on Stone Mountain."[120] While Borglum was never an official member of the Klan, he did attend rallies and served on organizational committees. After ten years of work, he was fired from the project in 1925 due in part to his ego and "delusion of

[119] Bernard, "The Creator of Mount Rushmore's Forgotten Ties to White Supremacy."
[120] Ibid.

grandeur," according to the committee that backed the project.[121] Those delusions also carried over to Rushmore, where he intended for the Constitution and the Declaration of Independence to be stored inside of the mountain as well.

*****

Rep. Ross originally wanted to ask for $5 million to pay Greenwood survivors. At that time, there were about one hundred people who were still alive by the time the report was released.[122] He also wanted $1 million for children's programs. He, along with Senator Maxine Horner, put their faith in the commission with the hope that it would find enough evidence to warrant a payment. The commission voted 7-4 to recommended payments to survivors (but did not suggest an amount), a memorial, and business incentives for Black residents as well as a scholarship program.[123] Because the commission had no legislative authority, it could only give recommendations, not requirements. Oklahoma State House Representative from Lawton, Abe Deutschendorf, wasn't the biggest fan of the commission's recommendation. He and State Senator Robert V. Malacek were fearful that granting reparations would set a precedent for other communities to seek payment.[124]

This was also the fear Florida lawmakers had when granting payments and benefits for Rosewood. The difference, however, was

---

[121] Ibid.

[122] Krehbiel, *Tulsa 1921*, 212.

[123] Ibid.

[124] Yardley, "Panel Recommends Reparations in Long-Ignored Tulsa Race Riot."

the messaging. To get the support of conservatives, supporters of the law avoided the conversation about race; instead the focus was about the loss of property rights and how the government neglected to protect its citizens.[125]

In 2003, a lawsuit was filed against the City of Tulsa and the State of Oklahoma for civil rights violations related to the massacre by the Tulsa Reparations Coalition. In Oklahoma, there's typically a two-year limitation for filing cases of this nature, but the attorneys who brought the suit said that the rule didn't apply because of the cover-up directly after the attack. The case was dismissed by the 10th Circuit Court of Appeals and ultimately dismissed by the Supreme Court in 2005.[126]

The fight for reparations in Tulsa, however, is not over. In May 2020, on the eve of the massacre's ninety-ninth anniversary, the Human Rights Watch released a lengthy report calling for reparations. The report also calls for specific actions including: [127]

- The recovery of remains from the mass graves
- Burial services and medical benefits
- Educational benefits and scholarships
- Economic development and investment in the affected community
- Subsidization of home mortgages and rent for long-term residents of Greenwood
- Private sector support

---

125 Samuels, "After Reparations."

126 Brown, "Human Rights Watch Calls for Tulsa Race Massacre Reparations."

127 Heath, "The Case for Reparations in Tulsa, Oklahoma."

As in the 1990s, the topic around reparations on a national level had become popular again, this time reaching the political sphere in 2019. On Juneteenth of that year, the House Judiciary Subcommittee on the Constitution, Civil Rights, and Civil Liberties held its first congressional hearing on reparations for the first time in nearly ten years. Unlike Oklahoma and Florida, which studied their respective incidents and produced a report, the US Congress at this point had refused to even study the case for reparations or the impact of slavery. HR 40, the Commission to Study and Develop Reparation Proposals for African Americans Act, had been repeatedly introduced on the floor for more than thirty years but never passed.

During this time, just a few miles away, Georgetown University established a reparations fund for the descendants of the 272 slaves the school owned. During the 2020 Democratic primary, reparations became a central topic for many of the candidates. New Jersey Senator Cory Booker introduced a companion to HR 40 in the Senate. The renewal of interest in the topic of reparations was sparked when journalist Ta-Nehisi Coates wrote "The Case for Reparations" in 2014 for *The Atlantic*.[128] It's difficult to determine whether or not reparations will be granted from the national level for the legacy of slavery. But again, there may be some evidence of hope at the state and local level. In 2020, the city of Asheville, North Carolina, voted to approve reparations for its Black residents.[129] The city council voted to provide funding to promote homeownership and business opportunities but stopped short of giving out direct payments. Surprisingly, the measure was passed by a unanimous

---

[128] Brown, "Human Rights Watch Calls for Tulsa Race Massacre Reparations."
[129] Vigdor, "North Carolina City Approves Reparations."

decision. The city has about 93,000 residents, 12 percent of whom are Black. Additionally, the mayor of Providence, Rhode Island, Jorge Elorza, signed an executive order to pursue "truth-telling" and a "reparations process."[130]

These cases throughout the country have shown that reparations are not only possible but necessary to repair past damages. We also know that unless a damaging event has been properly repaired that issues will persist, no matter how far in the past the incident may have occurred. Like a hurricane that has passed, while the storm may have stopped, the debris will remain until someone organizes the resources to clean it up.

Additional Policy Fixes

In addition to the ideas stated earlier, Tulsa may be able to adopt some of the following strategies that have been proposed at the national level.

Baby bonds

This was originally proposed by Cory Booker in 2018. Baby bonds, also known as the American Opportunity Accounts program, has four simple tenets.

1. Every child born would receive $1,000 to start.
2. Through the tax code, kids would receive up to $2,400 depending on family income.
3. The money would grow at 3 percent each year in a low-risk account managed by the US Treasury.

[130] List, "Providence Mayor Signs Order to Pursue Truth, Reparations."

4. The money couldn't be used by an individual until age eighteen. At that point, the money could be used only for education, homeownership, or retirement.

Based on how wealth is currently distributed, Black children will receive $29,000 compared to white children, who would receive $16,000. The numbers would be different if a plan like this were implemented at the city level, but because racial wealth disparities still exist in Tulsa, it's more likely that Black children would benefit more from this type of program.

Encourage businesses to spend in Black communities

Similar to the reparations in Asheville, Tulsa could opt to put laws on the books to encourage companies to invest in its Black residents. We know, unlike baby bonds, that this proposal can work on a city level. In the 1970s, Atlanta mayor Maynard Jackson mandated that 25 percent of construction contracts be set aside for businesses of color. According to the Greenlining Institute, that resulted in $1.6 billion dollars being awarded to minority firms.

Additionally, the city could encourage its largest businesses to direct a portion of their operating budget, money that was already earmarked to be spent, to Black businesses and Langston University-Tulsa, the state's only historically Black university.

Incentivize Black business ownership

The thing that made the Greenwood District special was its focus on entrepreneurship. Hotels, hospitals, theaters, grocery stores—all Black owned. To rebuild this, the local government could work to incentivize Black business owners by providing zero interest or forgivable loans. As the push to legalize marijuana became more mainstream, there have been several cities that have worked to provide a degree of reparations to those who were incarcerated due to marijuana possession or sales. In 2019, city officials in Evanston, Illinois wanted to levy a tax on legal marijuana sales to fund race-based reparations for its Black residents, ones who were most affected by the War on Drugs.[131] The City of Los Angeles in 2018 launched a program to grant licenses to residents if they met certain criteria, which included living in an area that was disproportionately targeted by police or having been previously arrested on a marijuana charge.[132] A similar mechanism could be useful in spurring entrepreneurship among Tulsa's Black residents. Just like the policies of the War on Drugs, the massacre in 1921 specifically targeted one group of people; the remedy to that problem will need to be just as targeted. In conjunction with any efforts to help encourage business owners, there should be a strong educational component to ensure that recipients are put in the best possible positions to succeed.

Individual Fixes

While large policy changes can help repair the damages that have happened in the past, it's important to note that Black Wall Street was built and maintained primarily through the effort and dedication of individuals. Reparations can help accelerate these individual efforts and increase the likelihood of success, lowering the degree of difficulty. Below are a few ideas that could be implemented on

---

[131] Armus, "A Chicago Suburb Wants to Give Reparations to Black Residents."
[132] Levin, "'This Was Supposed to be Reparations'."

an individual, family, and community level that could help rebuild Black Wall Street. Part II of this book will further discuss these ideas and provide more detail and analysis to create one's own personal wealth plan.

Reassess the value of real estate

In the Black community, there's a perception that real estate is at the top of the wealth food chain, the cornerstone at which wealth is created. While real estate is an important part of anyone's portfolio, African Americans should take a more measured approach. Real estate is an illiquid asset, meaning that when a portion needs to be sold it's not easy to do so. One cannot sell a portion of a home to pay for an emergency, and the buying and selling process can take weeks or months. More importantly, however, the real estate market is where African Americans are discriminated against the most and was one of the primary reasons why Black households didn't recover from the 2008 financial crisis.

By 2012, the median net worth for white families was down 16 percent compared to 50 percent for Black families. We know that this happened for two reasons: First, Black homes are devalued by $48,000 per home, which amounts to $156 billion in combined losses. Second, African Americans weren't investing in the stock market and didn't benefit from what would be the largest bull market in US history. Dorothy Brown, professor at Emory University Law School, stated in her 2012 *Forbes Magazine* article that in order for Black people "to have more wealth at home, we need to start investing outside of it."[133]

---

[133] Brown, "How Home Ownership Keeps Blacks Poorer Than Whites."

Employ the stock market

The stock market is perhaps the most transparent and least discriminatory avenue to build wealth. According to the US Federal Reserve Board Survey of Consumer Finances in 2016, 60 percent of whites had money in retirement accounts versus only 34 percent of African Americans.[134] Retirement accounts include Individual Retirement Accounts (IRAs) and employer-sponsored plans like 401(k), 403(b), and TSP accounts. For individual stocks, 61 percent of whites own stocks versus just 31 percent for African Americans.[135] For decades, the stock market wasn't as accessible in the past as it is today thanks to a number of apps and significantly lower fees in the industry. It is now more feasible than ever to invest in the market.

While many may feel that the stock market is too risky due to the market's ability to change direction within minutes, it's important to note that from 2000 to 2019 the market was only down five times. Thus there's a 73 percent chance that the market will be positive in any given year. Going back to 1990, the market has been down only six times, and going all the way back to 1980, the market has only been negative seven times. Those years were 1981, 1990, 2000, 2001, 2002, 2008 and 2018. More than 82 percent of the time, the market has been positive.

Those who have felt that the stock market is too expensive should reconsider as well. While this may have been the case in the past where investment firms required their clients to have $100,000 or even $250,000 to meet with a financial advisor, you can now

---

[134] Ross, "The Racial Wealth Gap in America: Asset Types Held by Race."

[135] Ibid.

invest with $5, or even less. Had the average person invested $200 per month, which is just $50 per week, into an index fund from January 2000 to August 2020 (around when this book was written), that investor would have more than $175,000 today. This is despite three stock market crashes: the dot-com bust, the financial crisis in 2008, and the coronavirus pandemic. Those results would have occurred no matter who was investing and isn't subject to racial bias in the same way real estate or obtaining business funding is.

Strategic spending

Shawn D. Rochester provides a simple acronym for creating more than six million jobs and 1.4 million businesses in the Black community. He suggests getting a "PHD," which stands for purchase, hire, and deposit. To rebuild Black Wall Street, every individual would need to commit to purchasing items from Black businesses, hiring Black people, and ensuring that you deposit your money with a Black bank. He goes on to suggest that each of the companies that you do business with also purchase, hire, and deposit a portion of their money with the Black community as well.

To visualize this, imagine going to a restaurant. The PHD method would suggest that I: 1) purposely choose one that's Black owned; 2) that the restaurant employs Black people; and 3) that the business and I have a portion of our money deposited at a Black-owned bank. This was done in the 1920s by default, so these questions and this mode of thinking wasn't required. Today it will require more questioning and more effort on the part of the buyer, but it's something worth pursuing and asking both of yourself and of the businesses that you give your money to. I will point out, however, that this isn't a totally foreign concept in a modern context. Many businesses now, especially those in the restaurant sector, have adopted the organic and locally-sourced business model because people want to buy from small local farmers. You can also see this in companies that openly advertise their commitment to climate change. There isn't too much of a difference between that philosophy and Black business investment because, for the most part, we expect the businesses that we buy from to reflect a portion of our own values. And when enough consumers ask and expect this, businesses are very quick to display their support. Nike's support of Colin Kaepernick, Ben and Jerry's Ice Cream's support of Black Lives Matter very early on, or Netflix's $100 million commitment to Black organizations are examples of companies that do this to a degree already.

Black Wall Street was designed and created with intention but was also a product of the era in which Jim Crow and white supremacy forced collective action. Black Wall Street can exist and thrive today, but we will need a much different blueprint to yield the same positive results for personal wealth and social mobility.

PART II:

CREATING, GROWING, AND PROTECTING BLACK WEALTH

As I learned bits and pieces about the Tulsa Race Massacre, I was always haunted by the question of how money worked. How was wealth created and how could that wealth be created again? What did our ancestors do? What tools did they have that we did not? It was these same questions that propelled me to become a financial advisor and found my own financial education company in 2010. That drive for answers helped me to manage more than $140 million as an advisor and be named among Investopedia's top 100 most influential financial advisors by 2017. For me, these overarching questions were born from a nagging curiosity rather than a feeling of not having enough as a child. My family was solidly middle-class; my father was a career firefighter, my mother worked at a local bank, and my stepfather worked for an airline in maintenance.

My father, an avid reader, would often go into seemingly random lectures about the importance of financial freedom, owning a business, and obtaining multiple streams of income. This wasn't just something he talked about; it was something that he modeled for me and my brother. In addition to his job as a firefighter, he taught CPR classes to local daycares and small businesses. In the early 2000s, he owned *Green Pages*, a directory for Black-owned businesses in Tulsa. As a kid, you pick up bits and pieces of your parent's lectures. It isn't until you run into a challenge that you find out whether or not you've learned anything. I was forced to begin applying those financial lessons on February 4, 2007.

That was the night of Super Bowl XLI, Peyton Manning's Indianapolis Colts versus the Chicago Bears. I got into a car wreck while leaving a friend's house after the game. No one was injured but that event did change the course of my life and how I viewed money. Prior to this point, I saw money as a byproduct of work, that the only way to obtain money was to trade time. After that wreck, I was forced to see things much differently. The car, a green 2002 Cadillac Eldorado, was totaled. Because I was the primary mode of transportation for my brother and I to get to and from school and my parents typically left for work early, it was imperative that I find a way to fix the situation, and quickly.

The solution to this problem came in the form of a job as a janitor, cleaning libraries across the city. Starting at about 10:00 p.m., I would meet up with the staff and drive to one of the libraries three nights a week, ending my shift between midnight and 1 a.m. This experience had a profound impact for two reasons.

First, I learned what I didn't want to do with my life. The job forced me to expand my view on what I wanted to be and where I wanted to be in the future. There was one man I worked with who was likely in his late fifties or early sixties. We'll call him Roy. Each night at the end of our shift, we had to sign a document that let the library staff know what was cleaned and if we found any problems or issues. I hadn't noticed it at first, but every night Roy would either pass the form to me or someone else to sign off. He later revealed that he never actually learned how to read but that he did recognize his name when written down. I knew at that moment that I didn't want to be stuck in any situation because of money. I quickly realized that money wasn't just a result of work, but it was a tool, something that buys choices. In that moment, neither of us had a real choice. I had to work because I needed the money to get a new car and it was one of very few options available. If I'd had more money, I could have had more options. Perhaps I could have bought another used car in cash or better insurance and avoided working nights altogether.

The second lesson was even more profound. While cleaning the offices at the Tulsa Central Library downtown, I came across *The Automatic Millionaire* by David Bach. Due to my curiosity around money, I was naturally attracted to the title. I found myself reading sections during our breaks and would pick up reading every night in different libraries. It was the very first time I read about money and how it was created. It was the first time I learned that there's a process to wealth and that it isn't something that happened by accident or luck. But the more I reflected on this experience as I have gotten older, I realized the importance of access and ability. Much like myself, Roy was exposed to the exact same information I had every night.

He had the answer to any question he could ever have among thousands and thousands of books. He had the access, but he didn't have the ability to use this access to his advantage. I learned that wealth creation is delicate. Someone with high income can easily squander an opportunity without the right tools, and there are times where simple hard work and discipline don't result in financial independence. There are systemic barriers that work to suppress wealth creation, particularly among the Black community, and it takes special knowledge, skill, and application to be financially successful.

In the following section of the book, I want to give readers a clear template to build wealth while also exposing the barriers that have worked to suppress Black wealth for decades.

CHAPTER 7:

THE $16 TRILLION PRICE TAG OF RACISM

To put it bluntly, racism is expensive, but in the United States the cost is shared, not just among Black Americans but by the United States as a whole. There are four key areas where these costs and disparities can be found: education, income, housing, and investing. Had the gaps in this area been closed just twenty years ago, the United States could have added $16 trillion to the economy.[136]

Obtaining an education was widely seen as the great equalizer in the Black community. But the data doesn't support this, especially when you factor in the cost of education and the differences in pay after graduation. Today, Black women are the most educated demographic in America. Black women made up 68 percent of associate's degrees, 66 percent of bachelor's degrees, and 71 percent of master's degrees between 2009 and 2010.[137] But due to racial and gender pay gaps, Black women only earn sixty-one cents for every dollar that a white man makes in the same job with the same

[136] Peterson, "Closing the Racial Inequality Gaps."

[137] Osbourne, "Black Women Become Most Educated Group in US."

qualifications. At this rate, Black women will not receive full pay equity until the year 2119, which is sixty-four years after white women are expected to reach pay equity in 2055.[138] Both Black men and Black women take on student debt at higher rates for college as well, meaning Black people are paying more and receiving less. Unfortunately, this theme of paying more and receiving less will become a painfully recurring theme.

Like most systemic issues, there are several intricate layers that can reinforce the cycle of racism. The education field is no different: At the K-12 level, the funding gap between minority school districts and white districts in the United States is $23 billion, despite serving the same number of students according to Citi.[139] This is because nearly every state relies on property taxes to fund education. As we've already established, Black homes are already devalued, which leaves a smaller tax base to fund schools in Black neighborhoods. Additionally, property taxes are only raised from those who own homes, not renters, and Black homeownership rates are 30 percent lower than white homeownership rates.[140] Again, African Americans end up paying more for less. On average, even when adjusting for the same credit score, Black people are paying a higher cost to own a home that is devalued, which then results in lower funding for education. If the gap in college degrees and advanced degrees were closed twenty years ago, it may have generated close to $113

---

[138] Thompson, "Despite Being the Most Educated, Black Women Earn Less Money."

[139] Peterson, "Closing the Racial Inequality Gaps."

[140] Choi, "Breaking Down the Black-White Homeownership Gap."

billion dollars in additional income, savings, and investment. This in turn would have resulted in 1.7 million additional Black college graduates.[141]

Perhaps the biggest driver in these disparities is the income gap. In the end, it is your income that allows one to save, invest, and establish financial stability. For obvious reasons, a lower income reduces the amount available to invest, own property, or start a business, and since wealth is a function of income, those lower inputs will produce lower wealth outputs. According to the 2020 Citi study *Closing the Racial Inequality Gaps*, "The Federal Reserve estimates that the wealth gap can be eliminated if the racial income gap is closed."[142] The problem, however, is that it could take 228 years for the gap to correct itself, barring a major policy fix.[143]

The housing sector is perhaps the most infamous for discriminating against African Americans. As recently as 2011, Bank of America paid $335 million in a lawsuit related to charging Black and Latinx homeowners higher interest rates and fees than white borrowers even though they had similar credit profiles. Charging minorities more to own a home is an unfortunate yet predictable American tradition going back to the mid-1930s, when the Federal Housing Administration (FHA) flat out refused to insure mortgages in and around Black neighborhoods. This process was known as redlining, and until 1968 it was legal. One study found that 98

[141] Peterson, "Closing the Racial Inequality Gaps."

[142] Peterson, "Closing the Racial Inequality Gaps."

[143] Davidson, "It Would Take 228 Years for Black Families to Amass Wealth of White Families."

percent of the FHA loans approved from 1934-1968 went to white applicants.[144] While this type of policy and social discrimination/bias was targeted at people of color, specifically African Americans, it still had a negative impact on the country as a whole. Had the nation improved access to housing credit for Black people, it could have added nearly 770,000 Black homeowners, adding $218 billion dollars in sales and expenditures over the past twenty years. This lost revenue only explodes if one could extrapolate the data back to the mid-1930s. One can only imagine the lost tax revenue local governments missed out on, the revenue that banks could have made as well as the financial strength that could have been passed on from generation to generation if equitable financial access had been granted to Black people.

It is exceedingly clear that the financial status of African Americans as a whole is a direct result of how the United States operates and treats its communities of color. Even with a long list of evidence to quantify how the wealth gap is created and why it still exists, there's still a prevailing belief for many that these statistics are more of a reflection of values for the African American community. Social media is littered with comments and memes that attempt to link occasional spending on luxury items like shoes or clothes to broader, more systemic outcomes. To put things more clearly, it's not purchasing a $200 pair of Jordans that created the wealth gap. The problem existed well before 1984 when the first shoe was released. To make significant progress in closing the wealth gap and creating financial stability for our communities, actionable education is key,

---

[144] Fulwood III, "The United States' History of Segregated Housing."

along with targeted policies as stated previously. While Black Wall Street was known for its collective economic strength, there must also be a strong individual financial platform to stand on. Policy and collective action with a solid personal financial foundation can place Black Americans in better position to not only start businesses but support them as well.

CHAPTER 8:

CREATING FINANCIAL STABILITY USING THE SIP SYSTEM

In 2016, while working as a financial advisor in New York City for two years, I started to notice a pattern among my wealthiest clients. Over my entire career as an advisor, I have interacted and advised no less than sixty millionaires, and even though they had different professional backgrounds and different styles of investing, coming from different corners of the country, the majority of them had the exact same foundational items besides income that allowed them to amass more than $1,000,000 in net worth. Using those findings, I began to create my own framework for building wealth.

I was able to summarize that foundation into one simple acronym—SIP—which stands for Save, Invest, Protect. Every financial tool that exists is to help you in one or more of these areas. Before going deeper into the SIP System, I want to discuss the importance of having a template or framework such as this to apply to your situation. Income is an important factor in building wealth, but it's not the only determinant of financial success. Without the right foundation and strategy in place, high-income earners will lose the money they've accumulated, but it is also important to note that wealth doesn't always have to be a specific dollar amount. Wealth can also be determined by the amount of time you can spend doing the things that you enjoy. The SIP System as well as other tools that I will provide can be applied with any income amount. As you will learn in this section, each of the three pillars is extremely important and missing just one will risk not only your financial future but may also have a negative impact on those who are around you as well. Even those with multimillion-dollar fortunes will see their wealth evaporate if each of these three areas isn't properly addressed.

Save

"Pay yourself first" is perhaps the oldest rule in the financial playbook, but it's still among the most important. Instead of drawing out the same old adages about the importance of paying yourself first, I will provide a few key strategies to help execute this in a more efficient way. The Federal Reserve found that the median savings balance for African Americans is $10,479, compared to $33,879 for whites. Recall that the median, by definition, is that half of the population has over that amount while the other half has under that amount. The average balance for African Americans was just $1,500. Yes, this is a reflection of the income gap, but there are still some important strategies that can and should be implemented. The median household income for Black families is about $46,073, according to the Economic Policy Institute.[145] Using that number, one could roughly estimate the monthly take-home pay after taxes to be somewhere around $2,700 per month.*

[145] Wilson, "Racial Disparities in Income and Poverty Remain Largely Unchanged."

*Tax rates will vary depending on family size, tax credits, location, and a number of other factors.

Because most experts would recommend at least six months of emergency savings, the median savings for Black families should be closer to $16,125. (We reach this number by taking one month of your take-home pay and multiplying by six.)

For those who feel that this number may be daunting, I have two suggestions:

1. This is not a figure that will be reached immediately. While it is important to prioritize this number, it may realistically take more than a year. That's okay as long as you're progressing.
2. One of the easiest ways to achieve a higher savings rate is to reverse engineer your living expenses. Let's assume that you want to build your emergency savings over a period of two years. If your goal is $16,125, dividing this number by twenty-four months would give you about $672 per month. If you are paid on a biweekly basis, this comes out to $336 for each paycheck. If at all possible, I would build this figure into my budget and begin making decisions around this number.

For example, anytime I was searching for an apartment or home, I made sure to include this number first and find housing that I can afford with this number included. If my take-home salary is $2,700 per month, then I view it as having only $2,028 left over to spend because I have paid myself first. Rent, student loans, day care, and other expenses will need to fall under that number, or very close to it.

If I cannot do this, then I have a few options. I could stretch the goal from two years to three years to lower the amount saved each month but still hit the same goal. I could find areas to cut or rearrange my other expenses, like choosing a different student loan payment plan or negotiating for better prices on certain services. Or I could find ways to increase my income by switching jobs or negotiating for a raise, or, if I'm an entrepreneur, raising my rates. Of all of the options, I prefer switching jobs as a way to maximize income. In 2019, *Forbes* reported that those who switch jobs see an average annual salary increase of nearly 10 percent compared to those who stayed, who saw on average a raise of 4 percent.[146]

Finally, to further build your savings, it's important to make sure this process is automated. Make sure to set up an automatic regular transfer from your checking account to a separate savings. This is key because you never want to confuse the money you need for bills with the money you need for savings and security. The automation piece is to help ensure that you're not relying on willpower to reach your goal. Your willpower can fail; your auto deposit will not. For those who don't have a regular income, you may want to opt for a percentage rather than a dollar amount to transfer. Instead of $336 every two weeks, perhaps 10-15 percent during that period is better. Again, the key here is about progress.

Invest

While building up a cash reserve is important, that alone will not be enough. Wealth is generated when you're able to employ your money to generate an income. To use a metaphor, a portion of your money should be clocking in Monday through Friday from

[146] Kelly, "New Study Concludes That it Literally Pays to Switch Jobs Right Now."

9:30 a.m. to 4:00 p.m. Work in this case is the stock market. As mentioned earlier, it has become one of the easiest ways to grow wealth regardless of budget. While it isn't the only way to invest, this will be our primary focus due to the advantages that we'll discuss in the next chapter.

On average, the stock market has returned about 7 percent annually after inflation. In a way you could consider this the "salary" that your money will be earning on your behalf. By sending $1,000 to "work" in the stock market for a year, I would be expecting $1,072.50 at the end of the year. By sending that money back to work in year two, I would have $1,150.26, and the process would continue. Because of compounding interest, the original $1,000 has generated $150.26. By contrast, if that same amount of money were left in a bank account at 1 percent, it would have only generated $20.20, more than seven times less.

It is important to note that the 7 percent figure is an average due to the nature of the stock market. Very rarely in any one year will you gain exactly 7 percent, and in fact there will be some years where you could lose money. The threat of loss and the history of mistreatment of Black people by financial institutions is well documented as previously discussed. To that point, it must also be recognized that among the Black community, the stock market is an underutilized tool that has now become much more accessible and has more than a hundred-year history of positive growth over the long-term.

The stock market shouldn't be treated as get-rich-quick solution or a lottery ticket. It should be seen more as a garden, something that's planted and routinely taken care of, growing over time. Expecting an immediate and significant return from the market is not the mindset most people should have. Doing so is like planting an apple seed and expecting fresh apple juice in ten minutes.

Is the market safe? Is now the time to invest?

The word "safe" will always be a relative term. What may be safe for some may be dangerous to others, but do recall the stat cited earlier, that since 1990 the stock market has been negative only six times. Had you invested $10,000 in 1990, you would have nearly $167,000 at the end of 2019 without ever adding any money. These types of returns aren't guaranteed in the future. However, the hundred-plus years of data that we do have should help soothe some concerns.

It is my position that "now" is always the right time to invest, but that what one chooses to invest in is highly dependent on that individual's tolerance for risk and what type of investments they choose to select. Investment selection in risk will be covered in the next chapter.

"I prefer to invest only in things I can see and touch."

I have witnessed a hesitancy to invest in the stock market among African Americans because of the lack of tangibility, meaning that you cannot touch and feel the investment in the same way you would real estate. I've often made the argument that this is not true, because if you own shares of Wal-Mart, you can walk into the store in the same way that you would walk into a business that you started on your own. When you invest in the stock market, you're a partial business owner, and that business produces products in the real world that you're likely to interact with on a regular basis. The stock market is not perfect, but it does offer three key advantages that physical investments do not. Each of these I will discuss in the next chapter.

Protect

The last item in the SIP System refers to the assets you've worked to build as well as the family members you wish to help succeed in the future. Primarily this protection piece revolves around a few tools: life insurance, wills, and beneficiaries. It also refers to the ways that you can protect your investments as well, and will be discussed in the next chapter. While this is not a comprehensive list, these are the primary tools needed to transition wealth efficiently from generation to generation. Not executing on this financial pillar, you're risking asset erosion, which means that the money that was intended to go to loved ones is significantly reduced due to legal fees, debts, and other expenses that weren't properly planned for. Regardless of the level of wealth you currently have, the financial pillar of protection will always be important. We've seen several celebrity cases with tens of millions of dollars lost or eroded by not properly protecting the money they worked so hard to build.

One of the most recent examples is Prince, when he died without a will in April 2016. At the time of his death, he was worth between $100 to $300 million. A will is an estate-planning tool that allows you to decide where your money, property, and other assets go at death. Without a will, your assets may take longer to go through the probate process, which can result in more fees and less money going to your heirs. As of writing, Prince's six siblings are entering year five of probate and have paid tens of millions of dollars to lawyers and consultants over that time. In addition to that, the IRS believes Prince's estate owes an additional $32.4 million in federal taxes and tacked on a $6.4 million penalty for undervaluing his assets.[147] While the average person will not experience the degree of complication that Prince's family is currently enduring, it does go to show that even with millions of dollars, these same principles of saving, investing, and protection must still be followed.

For the average person, probate can cost between 4-7 percent of the total estate value.[148] Having a will can help get your assets through probate a bit more quickly and reduce some of those fees, but outside of the financial cost, there's something to be said for the emotional burden that can be lifted when your wishes have been clearly expressed instead of the court system making those decisions among family arguments. In some cases, your state's law may allow you to use a handwritten will. However, I would caution against using this method. With the death of singer Aretha Franklin, three handwritten wills were discovered in her home in May 2019, several months after she died in August 2018. The most accurate approach is to consult an attorney that specializes in estate planning. The next best method of obtaining a will is by creating one using one of the online services listed in the resource section.

Wills are just one portion of the protection puzzle. Another important piece is your beneficiary designations. A beneficiary is the person (or persons) listed on your account(s) that will receive the funds upon your passing. Designating beneficiaries is one of the most powerful and efficient tools in wealth planning. This is because in most cases a beneficiary supersedes a will, bypasses the probate process, and may be transferred in a matter of days instead

---

[147] CBS News, "Prince's Estate Undervalued by About $80 Million."

[148] County of Santa Clara, "How to Probate a Decedent's Estate."

of weeks or months in comparison to probate. Beneficiaries can be designated on a number of different assets, but primarily you will find this option on retirement accounts like IRAs, 401(k)s ,403 (b)s, brokerage accounts, checking and savings accounts, and life insurance policies.

It is important to make sure that these beneficiaries are updated on a regular basis as your family situation may change over time. In fact, your entire financial plan should be adjusted any time you experience a major life event. This normally includes a death in the family, divorce, birth, marriage, or adoption. Making these periodic adjustments may help prevent passing the money to someone who's no longer living or no longer relevant, such as passing money to a former spouse or deceased family member. Additionally, if you have multiple children, you'll want to ensure that all of them are added, especially if there's a significant age gap between them. You could be risking leaving one or more children out of an inheritance due to this oversight.

Finally, you will want to employ life insurance as a key tool in protecting your wealth. For many who've explored life insurance options, they may have questioned the pros and cons of term life insurance versus permanent (also known as whole life insurance). I will not rehash that debate here, but I will say that the most important thing is having some level of coverage. Life insurance is one of the few ways that one can pass on wealth without taxation. Life insurance can also be a very useful tool to take care of final expenses beyond just funeral costs but estimated taxes on potential assets such as real estate or even continuing a business after a partner has passed. I've had some clients use life insurance as a hedge for their home; if one spouse were to pass, the remaining spouse had enough money to pay off their home. This means that the spouse and family could live more comfortably and wouldn't strain to keep up with expenses. The other important feature of life insurance is that so long as the premiums are paid, the policy is guaranteed. That's not a feature that many financial instruments can deliver.

So, what are the major differences between term life insurance policies and permanent life insurance policies? When signing up for a term life insurance policy, you're locking yourself into a fixed payment for a specified term, in some cases twenty or thirty years. During that time, as long as payments are made, your family is guaranteed a certain amount if you pass within the term. Term life insurance is generally much less expensive than whole life, but advocates of term life insurance argue that the difference in payment between the two types of policies could be invested, and therefore the term life insurance holder will have more money in the end. The argument here is that if someone opts for a term life insurance policy and they are investing during that term, then once the time has expired, they should have enough money to self-insure at that point in time, or the items you were protecting against, like a home, will be paid off.

On the opposite end, the argument for a whole life is the policyholder is covered for their entire life, as the title suggests. While these policies are usually much more expensive than term policies, the argument is that whole life insurance has additional benefits that are worth more than the increased price. For example, many argue that the cash value that accumulates with the policy is a significant feature. In a whole life policy, cash value is essentially a built-in savings account that earns interest as you're making payments to the policy. This money could be used to withdraw or borrow against in the event of an emergency or as an additional way to save for retirement.

Both claims are true, but there's a very important distinction that I wish to make. A whole life policy should not be seen as a primary retirement vehicle. While it can be used as one, it is among the least efficient options. Attempting to use any life insurance policy as your primary retirement asset is like using a cell phone to write a novel. Is it possible? Yes. Is it the easiest, most efficient way to do so? No, not at all. It makes much more sense to prioritize 401(k) plans and individual retirement accounts first. Both accounts give you the potential to achieve a much higher growth rate and with the 401(k) you may be eligible for a company match depending on where you work, which is a benefit no other investing option can offer. If you have contributed the maximum amount to those accounts, then a whole life policy may be an option. If you have not maxed out on those accounts, I would not consider looking at a whole life policy. Also remember that there are fees associated with any insurance policy, but those fees are magnified in a whole life policy. You will need to take a very hard look to compare the cost you're paying for the benefit that you may be receiving and compare that to how that money could be growing with other investment options.

In what order should one go about executing the SIP System? The most important thing is to protect yourself and make sure, for any existing accounts, that the beneficiaries are up to date, that you have a life insurance policy in place, and a will. It's important to protect the assets you currently have in case the unforeseen does occur, as time is not promised. The protection piece in my view is also one of the easiest tasks to manage and is much more of a set-it-and-forget-it process, meaning that once the beneficiary is set and the will is complete, they're pretty much done. While you can always go back and make changes, it's not something that needs to be monitored on a regular basis like other items.

After the protection is established, I would then move toward savings, followed by investing. Admittedly, these two categories can happen at the same time and you do not need to wait to hit your ultimate savings goal to start investing. In fact, waiting for years to begin investing is one of the costliest financial mistakes a person can make. This is because compounding interest relies on time; the longer you invest the more your money grows. For example, if your goal is to have $1 million by age sixty-seven, you will need to invest $214 per month at a 9 percent interest rate if you begin at age twenty-seven. Waiting until age thirty-seven, it goes up to $541 per month. At age forty-seven, it will cost $1,491, and $5,168 by fifty-seven. A better way to accomplish this is to prioritize the savings more while still contributing some amount to your investing goals. Once the savings goal is reached, you can devote more to your investing efforts.

CHAPTER 9:

NAVIGATING THE STOCK MARKET AND GENERATIONAL WEALTH

There are dozens of reasons as to why African Americans are not participating in the stock market at a higher rate. Those reasons include the sobering fact that less than 5 percent of all financial advisors are Black.[149] The lack of Black advisors speaks to lack of access and the history of how financial institutions have worked to hurt the interests of Black people for years. When I was interviewing to become a financial advisor in 2014, I learned very quickly how rare it was to see people like me. It was never a career field that I was aware of. My parents never had a financial advisor, nor was there one in our family; I was the first. I also learned firsthand how systemic issues weighed much heavier on Black financial advisors and forced many out of the advisory role.

Financial advising, more than many other fields, is about building relationships. This is magnified because people are trusting you with their money and future. When you're sitting in that chair and creating a financial plan, choosing investments, and helping to

[149] Malito, "Three Reasons You Don't See Many People of Color in the Financial Services Industry."

grow and protect someone's wealth, they have to trust you and your judgment. So just like other fields, people rely on recommendations and social cues to find those trusted individuals. It's much easier to trust someone who looks like you, talks like you, and understands your experience. But the added layer is the fact that most financial advisors, to be profitable, must focus on clients with a certain net worth and due to the wealth and income gap we know that those people tend to be white. White clients with money are more likely to choose a white advisor whom a family member recommended or who lives in their neighborhood. This does not make a Black advisor's job impossible, but it makes it much more difficult for two reasons: The first is that when going into those white spaces, you may be treated as "the other," or as less trustworthy or less intelligent simply because of your skin color. Second, the opposite end of the spectrum also presented challenges. Because of the perception of financial institutions in the Black community, Black advisors in my experience had to combat years of mistrust and skepticism around investing in assets that were not tangible. After that, Black advisors would need to acquire a larger amount of clients because of the lower average level of wealth held by Black clients. The median retirement balance for whites was $79,500. For African Americans, it was approximately 2.7 times less, at $29,200.[150]

I realized at perhaps the most inconvenient time how different things were in finance for Black people. In the summer of 2014, I moved to the Saint Louis area for a nine-month financial advisor training program. If you recall, this was around the same time that protests were in full swing due to the death of Michael Brown by

---

[150] Wills, "Retirement Savings by Race."

the Ferguson Police Department. Our training program placed an emphasis on client acquisition, and the primary method of doing this was by going door-to-door. I instantly realized that even in a suit and tie the rules were going to be very different for me, especially considering the fact that the company often highlighted key neighborhoods that had the highest incomes. Those areas were usually white and posed a much greater threat for me than they did for white advisors in my class. In situations like this, options are slim. Either go to the neighborhoods in which you're most comfortable and be okay working two times or even three times as hard for the same results or risk your life attempting to play by a set of rules that weren't written for people like you.

During this program, we would have speakers share their experience from the field periodically. There was one gentleman's story that stood out and really crystallized how different things were for people who looked like me. The man began his story talking about the traits needed to be successful at the company. The trait he was most proud of was persistence. He told us about a story where he walked up to a prospect's front door and knocked. After coming to the door, the prospect quickly shut the door in his face. Instead of walking away, discouraged, he told us that he hopped the back fence and knocked on his back door. As the story goes, the prospect was so enamored by his persistence that he then became his best client. After that moment, I knew that I would never benefit from that level of privilege in any point in history but especially in the context of Ferguson, MO, in 2014. I needed to find as many Black advisors as possible and learn from their experience in order to find a more feasible route to success in this field.

But even finding Black financial advisors was a difficult task. Thankfully for both Black investors and Black advisors, the landscape has significantly changed since then.

In the past, investment companies were focused primarily on high net worth clients, usually those with $250,000 or more (which again skewed to be more white), and compensation was based on commission. This model wasn't suitable to the average Black investor because it forced advisors to ignore them in search for wealthier potential clients and higher commissions. Today, the financial advisory sector is much more focused on charging a flat fee, meaning that anyone, regardless of the amount of money they have, can seek out a financial advisor instead of being instantly turned away because you don't have a certain asset level. For the Black advisor, this makes things easier as well because you aren't incentivized to only target wealthier whiter clientele. Instead, you can now focus on the clients whom you love working with most because all clients are going to bring in the exact same amount of revenue.

Another welcomed change to the financial space is the number of financial influencers and authors that have emerged in the past ten years. Prior to this, the majority of financial advice you would find on TV or in a bookstore didn't really account for the challenges that people of color would face. Due to the rising cost of college and the increasing burden of student loans, there was a large outcry from the personal finance community, mostly white, that suggested that if college couldn't be paid in cash that you shouldn't go. The problem is that for Black people, this creates an even bigger systemic problem. Yes, right now the cost of college is far too high and there should be measures to curtail that, but certain professions, like doctors, lawyers, and pharmacists, are needed in the Black community. Those professions require a college degree and, because they are advanced in nature, generally require a significant amount of money, money that often isn't sitting in cash or passed down from generation to generation. If the entire Black community followed that line of thinking, there would be no Black lawyers, no Black judges, and no Black doctors, yet data has shown how important it is to have Black people represented in those professions. As of 2020, though Black Americans make up 13 percent of the US population, only 5 percent of physicians are Black.[151] One study shows that having a Black doctor can reduce the Black-white gap in cardiovascular mortality among males by 19 percent and create an 8 percent decline in the Black-white male life expectancy gap.[152] For Black women, having a Black doctor, especially during pregnancy, can mean the difference between life and death. Black women are three to four times more likely to die during childbirth. According to an NPR story, "33 percent of black women said that they personally had been discriminated against because of their race when going to a doctor or health clinic, and 21 percent said they have avoided going to a doctor or seeking health care out of concern they would be racially discriminated against."[153] These larger systemic issues are not on the mind of a typical financial educator but are on the minds of Black financial educators and advisors, and not including these perspectives can be dangerous for African Americans as a whole.

*****

[151] NPR, "The Importance of Black Doctors."
[152] National Bureau of Economic Research, "Does Diversity Matter for Health."
[153] NPR, "The Importance of Black Doctors."

Why is investing in the stock market the key to generational wealth?

I've been on record for a number of years stating that the stock market is not the most perfect investment vehicle, that it has its disadvantages. While this is true, every investment option, whether it be real estate, opening your own business, or buying a franchise, has a certain level of risk and disadvantage. I have been consistent, however, in my belief that the stock market is the most convenient, most accessible, most flexible, and most equitable option out there.

Before laying out and explaining my method of investing in the market and creating financial independence and generational wealth, I first want to espouse why I'm favoring the stock market over other investing options.

#1 The Stock Market Is Liquid

Liquidity means that you're able to convert an investment into cash very quickly. For example, if you owned a stock and sold it for a profit, you could have the money in hand in less than five business days. You also wouldn't have to sell the entire investment. You could choose to sell only a portion of your investment and leave the rest to grow. In real estate, this isn't always the case. If you were buying a home or renting a home out, you couldn't simply sell off a room, and even in real estate transactions, it's exceedingly rare that the funds would be available in less than a week. Owning assets that are liquid allows you to be more flexible and respond to challenges and opportunities more quickly.

#2 The Stock Market Is More Accessible

Compared to most investing options, the stock market offers a very low entry point, and with the trends that are occurring in the investing space, that entry point has never been lower. Real estate can often require significant down payments as well as credit checks and income verification before acquiring the property. A down payment alone for some can be tens of thousands of dollars. Comparatively, owning a franchise like a McDonald's will cost millions just to get started. But in contrast, you can begin participating in the stock market for as little as $5, and in some cases less. For obvious reasons, the larger amount that you put into the market, the larger your returns, but even smaller dollar amounts like $50 or $100 per month can grow significantly depending on what you choose to invest in.

#3 The Stock Market Is Less Expensive

In most cases, investing in the stock market is less expensive in terms of fees. For example, in 2019 the sandwich franchise Subway charged a $15,000 franchise fee with start-up costs ranging between $116,000 and $263,000. McDonald's is significantly more expensive at $45,000 for the franchise fee with start-up expenses being north of $2 million. Real estate often has related maintenance costs and interest fees like property tax, closing costs, and maintenance. This is not to say that investing in the stock market has no fees at all. Many retirement funds do charge some fees within the investment itself, and those should be considered.

CHAPTER 10:

BASIC INVESTING TERMS YOU NEED TO KNOW

As someone who has been in the financial education space for more than a decade, I often hear about how the vocabulary of the stock market is intimidating. As we move into the next section on investing, I want to take the time to decode some of the more common investing terms that we'll discuss.

For context, I define retirement and financial freedom as the point at which your job becomes optional. With that, we'll go into some of the most common tools you can use to reach financial freedom.

Retirement Accounts

401(k)

A 401(k) is a company-based investing account primarily for retirement. Each year you are able to contribute money up to the limit set by the IRS, which is periodically adjusted. In 2010, the limit for people under age 50 was $16,500, by 2015 it was $18,000 before rising to $19,500 in 2020. After age fifty, you're allowed to have a "catch-up" contribution; this number is usually adjusted as well. In 2019, it was $6,000 and went up to $6,500 in 2020.

A 401(k) is known as a tax-deferred account, meaning that the money going into the account isn't taxed. The tax payment that you would have incurred is deferred until you make a withdrawal. Generally, these withdrawals shouldn't occur until after age fifty-nine and a half. Unless you qualify under certain rules, withdrawing before fifty-nine and a half will result in a penalty plus taxes. Compared to other retirement accounts, like an Individual Retirement Account (IRA), the 401(k) allows you to invest significantly more money. Today you can contribute nearly three times more in a 401(k) than you can in an IRA. An additional feature of a 401(k) is that some companies will match the funds you contribute to the account. This is a very powerful wealth-building feature that's not available with other vehicles. Generally you cannot own individual stocks inside of a 401(k); your investment choices are usually limited to the options provided by the employer and usually only include a set of mutual funds.

Traditional IRA

A traditional Individual Retirement Account is a retirement account that you can open on your own for the purpose of retirement. This account is also tax-deferred but as mentioned earlier, has a much lower contribution limit and catch-up contribution limit. Like the 401(k), those contribution limits have periodically increased over the years. From 2013 to 2018, the contribution limit was just $5,500 per year and jumped to $6,000 in 2019. The catch-up contributions for those over age fifty had been just $500 from 2002 to 2005, and was bumped up to $1,000 per year after 2006.

One of the important distinctions between individual retirement accounts and employer retirement accounts like the 401(k) is that you have more investment options available to you. In the next subsection, I will describe each of those investing options and how they fit into each account.

Roth IRA

There are a few key differences between a traditional IRA and a Roth IRA. The first is that a Roth IRA is funded with post-tax money. This means that money you deposit into this account has already been taxed. If you hold the account for at least five years and you are fifty-nine and a half, you would be able to withdraw the money without taxes or penalty. It is one reason why the Roth IRA is such a powerful investing tool. However, it's not for everyone; the IRS has an income limit for those who are able to open and contribute to this type of account. As with most tax numbers and IRS rules, this income limit is adjusted on a periodic basis and also depends on your tax filing status. Finally, another differentiating feature for the Roth IRA is that you're able to withdraw the money that you contributed to the account at any time. In a 401(k) and traditional IRA, the money you contribute to those accounts cannot be touched in most cases without a penalty, but because the money in a Roth IRA has already been taxed, you're allowed to withdraw the amount you deposited without those ramifications. Still, the interest on that original amount would be penalized if withdrawn. Both a traditional and Roth IRA may hold stocks, ETFs, mutual funds, bonds, and other types of investments.

Brokerage Account

A brokerage account is a basic investing account that you can use for almost any purpose. There are no income limits, contribution limits, or special tax benefits like retirement accounts. If you sell an investment for a profit, you may have a taxable event. Like IRAs, a brokerage account may hold any of the investing options listed below.

529 Savings Plan

A 529 plan is a tax advantage investing account primarily for the cost of education. Money that goes into this account and used for qualified education expenses is allowed to grow tax free and withdrawn tax free. 529 plans may not invest in individual stocks and are only limited to the investments allowed by the brokerage company, which generally consist of mutual funds only.

Where can I open these accounts?

Go to BuildingBread.com/resources to get a list of the best places to open an investing account.

Types of Investments and Terms to Know

It's important to recognize that the investing account options that we've covered are not investments themselves. They are the tools through which you can buy stocks, ETFs, and other investments. Think of an investment account like an oven; if you're looking for a meal, you need to put food in the oven to begin cooking. In this case, the types of investments I've listed below would be the food. Once you open an account, it's your job to then deposit money and select the investment. If you don't select an investment, the money will sit there and not be put to work, potentially a very costly mistake.

Several years ago, I met a lady who was looking to retire within a few months. She had worked at a department store for more than twenty years and brought her 401(k) statements with her. As I was reviewing the statement, she said that she'd begun putting money away for years but wasn't exactly sure why the money hadn't grown. I quickly discovered that more than 90 percent of her money was in cash. For decades, she had a 401(k) and put thousands of dollars into it, but never selected an investment. The money had been sitting there essentially doing nothing. There are three parts to starting the investing process: Open the account, deposit the money, choose your investments.

Ticker Symbol

Stocks, ETFs, and mutual funds all have what are called a ticker symbol. This is a set of letters that identify the company or fund. For example, the ticker symbol for Apple is AAPL, Disney is DIS, Johnson and Johnson is JNJ, etc. Typing the ticker symbol into your investing app or website will pull up all the information and news for the investment.

Stock

A stock (sometimes called equity) represents a portion of ownership in a company. Much like a deed or title to a car proves that you're the owner of that asset, a stock means that you own a portion of the company. Units of stocks are known as shares and shares can be in wholes or fractions. For example, you may own one share of a company or hundreds of shares. The number of shares denotes the amount of money that you've invested. The price of a stock will change during the market hours of 9:30 a.m. and 4:00 p.m. Eastern time. Those daily fluctuations are due to investor sentiment, news, and overall company health.

Stocks are bought and sold on exchanges. Think of investing like a road trip. The car is your investing account. This is the vehicle you're using to get you to the destination of financial freedom. That makes your stocks (as well as other investments listed below) the gas that propels the car forward, allowing things to move. But you can only get gas at a gas station; this is your stock market exchange. The primary exchanges in the United States are the New York Stock Exchange and NASDAQ.

Examples include: Wal-Mart (WMT), Procter and Gamble (PG).

ETF

ETF stands for exchange traded fund. ETFs have the ability to hold multiple stocks at one time. Like stocks, the price of an ETF will change frequently during the day. The advantage of ETFs, however, is that the risk is generally being spread out across dozens, sometimes hundreds of stocks, at a time. When explaining this to my students, I like to use the sports metaphor of choosing your favorite team, which would be one stock, versus the entire league, which will be owning an ETF. In any one year, you may assume that you know which team will be best. However, if you were to own the entire league, you do not risk being wrong and by default you're going to have the best team either way. For this reason, ETFs are known to be less risky than holding a single stock.

Examples include: SPDR Dow Jones Industrial Average (DIA), Invesco Nasdaq 100 (QQQ).

Mutual Fund

Mutual funds are very similar to ETFs, one of the key differences being how frequently the price changes during the day. The price change of a mutual fund is only reflected at the end of the trading day. In some cases, a company will offer the same investment but have an ETF version and a mutual fund version. For example, there's the Vanguard Total Stock Market Index Fund with the ticker symbol of VTSMX. There's also an ETF version of the Total Stock Market Index Fund with the symbol VTI. There are almost no differences in terms of the money you could make between the mutual fund version or the ETF version; however, mutual funds generally charge higher fees and may require a minimum to begin investing, whereas ETFs tend to charge much lower fees and have no minimums to start.

Examples include: Fidelity Strategic Dividend & Income Fund (FSDIX), T. Rowe Price Health Sciences Fund (PRHSX).

Index Fund

An index is a way of tracking the performance of a group of companies. An index fund tracks large segments of the stock market and invests in those companies. There are several indices, but the two most popular are the Standard and Poor's 500 index, also known as the S&P, and the Dow Jones industrial average. The S&P 500 tracks the five hundred largest companies in the United States, while the Dow Jones only tracks the performance of the US's thirty largest companies. An S&P 500 index fund would simply invest in all five hundred companies in the index. Index funds are known to have very low expenses and tend to be among the best options for most investors. An index fund is a type of ETF or mutual fund.

Finally, index funds are "the bar" against which most investments are measured. Stocks or funds that are considered to be "good" are those that have consistently beaten the index.

Examples include: Vanguard Total Stock Market Index Fund (VTSMX), iShares Expanded Tech-Software (IGV).

Bonds

A bond is an investment that represents a loan by an investor to an institution. Generally, this institution is usually a company or some level of government: state, federal or local. In exchange for this loan, the investor receives a fixed interest rate and at the end of the loan term receives the original principal. Bonds are known to be a counterweight to stocks in that when stocks tend to fall, bonds tend to rise because they are more solid and predictable and on the opposite end of things. When stocks tend to rise, bonds tend to fall because investors are looking for a much higher return. Investors primarily straddle both stocks and bonds at different rates as they age. It is also important to note that the average investor does not buy bonds on their own as they do with an individual stock. Most investors today are using bond funds like the Vanguard Total Band Market Index, which is an ETF.

Examples include: iShares Core US Aggregate Bond ETF (IGG), Vanguard Short-Term Corporate Bond Index ETF (VCSH).

REIT

A real estate investment trust is a company that owns and manages real estate properties. REITs like stocks and ETFs are traded on an exchange and can be bought and sold in the same way. REITs allow investors to own things like apartment buildings, hotels, office buildings, cell towers, and more. Generally, REITs are known for their stable dividend payments and sold returns.

Examples include: American Tower (AMT), Equinix (EQIX) & Digital Realty Trust (DLR).

Dollar Cost Averaging (DCA)

Dollar cost averaging is an investment strategy where an investor contributes a set amount of money on a periodic basis, typically on a biweekly, monthly schedule. By default, most retirement plans are already set up in this way because you're contributing a set percentage of your income. The purpose of DCA is to help avoid the mistake of mistiming the stock market and pouring money into an investment at the wrong time. Dividing the money and buying at different times helps you as an investor buy more when the price is low and less when the company is higher.

Dividend

A dividend is a payment that a company makes to its shareholders. Dividends can be a way to generate passive income from the stock market. There are some mutual funds and ETFs that only invest in dividend-paying companies. But know that just because a company doesn't pay dividends doesn't mean it isn't a good company. Whether or not a dividend is paid is based first on the financial health of the company; in some cases, if the business is under pressure dividends could be cut. The philosophy of the management team may also determine whether or not the money that could have been used for dividends is better off reinvested to continue growing the company.

Generally older, more established companies pay consistent dividends while many younger tech companies are more focused on aggressive growth and innovation.

Giving Your Money a Job

I view investing as giving your money a job, a place to work every day from 9:30 a.m. to 4:00 p.m. It is my job as the investor to make sure that every dollar is hired by the right companies or funds. For example, $100 of my money can go to work at Nike every day. Another $100 can go to work at an index fund. That money continues to grow and work harder every day so that real-life work increasingly becomes optional for me because my money goes to work every day.

The Seven Secrets of Investing Success

Over my career, with dozens of multimillion-dollar clients and more than 15,000 students, I've narrowed down seven key traits that successful investors have. Investors who tend to create generational wealth, avoid major losses, and employ their money effectively have all carried these traits. Use the following seven tips as a template to build from. For a more in-depth review of this process, go to BuildingBread.com/resources to view other wealth-building courses and guides that I've created.

1. Know Yourself as an Investor

The most important thing is knowing yourself as an investor. This means understanding your relationship with money and how you react when things aren't in your favor. Having a very clear answer to this question sets you up for success because it brings clarity to the things you should be investing in and also the things that you should avoid as an investor.

Here are just a few questions to ask yourself:

1. If the value of an investment drops by 30 percent in three months or less, what is your reaction? Will you continue holding that investment, would you buy more, or would you sell?
2. How long will you allow the money to grow before you consider using the proceeds?
3. Do you prefer an investment that has little to no fluctuation, and if so, are you willing to accept a lower gain?
4. What is the ultimate goal that you want to achieve?

While this isn't a comprehensive list of questions, it does help steer you in the right direction. Both in 2008 and in 2020, the stock market dropped more than 30 percent in less than three months. Investors who were willing to buy more or hold on could be considered undisciplined investors, or perhaps have a more long-term focus, but if your answer was to sell, then you may be a more conservative investor and prefer investments that are relatively stable and predictable. With all these questions, there's no right or wrong answer; however, the answers that you do have must align with the types of investments you'll eventually hold.

The second question is important because the time you have before you need the money (also known as the time horizon) has a significant impact on which investments may be most useful. As an example, we know that the stock market has the ability to generate the highest return in most cases; however, the shorter the time frame, the less predictable the market can be. If you can allow the money to grow for five years or more, investing in the stock market could make a lot of sense, but if you only had five days or five months, the chance that you can lose the money is significantly higher and investing in the market would not be wise. Something safer such as a savings account or certificate of deposit would be a much better option.

The third question is to help you understand your investing style. Some investments can be more volatile with big swings in either direction, while others are far more predictable but gain less. Essentially do you prefer to go slow and steady or swing for the fences every time? Someone who prefers this slow and steady approach might consider investing in a company like Johnson & Johnson, while someone who loves to swing for the fences might prefer a trendy technology company such as Apple. A sum of $1,000 invested in Johnson & Johnson from January 2010 to January 2021 would have grown to $3,150 for a gain of 251 percent. In contrast, the same $1,000 invested in Apple from January 2000 to January 2021 would be $20,760, nearly eight times higher than the money you would have made in Johnson and Johnson. Knowing that information, why would someone consider investing in a company that doesn't grow at the same rate as an entity like Apple? Stocks like Apple are known to take more significant losses from time to time while Johnson and Johnson's losses are, by comparison, much more mild. Studies have shown that the pain of losing money is psychologically twice as powerful as the joy of winning money. This plays out in other areas outside of money as well. People often remember the terrible hurricane, snowstorm, or wildfire that impacted us, but we don't often remember all of the perfect weather days, even though the number of those perfect days far outnumbers the times we've experienced a natural disaster. Those who aren't equipped to respond to dips in the market should instead invest in places that are less volatile and more reliable. Will these more conservative risk-averse investors make as much money? No, but they may be less stressed and sleep easier at night. Those characteristics are important because if you as an investor are overly stressed or emotional during the investing process, those emotions could force you into mistakes that cost you in the future.

In addition to the questions listed above, most investors will fall into one of the two following categories.

Passive Investor

If you know you're the set-it-and-forget-it type of investor, someone who prefers to deposit their money and put things on autopilot, then index funds are likely the most useful investing tool. Not only are index funds very inexpensive in terms of fees but are also very difficult to beat; in fact, more than 90 percent of professional investors fail to beat the index after fifteen years. This is one reason why one of the world's wealthiest men, Warren Buffett, recommends index funds. In 2007, John C. Bogle quoted Warren Buffett in *The Little Book of Common Sense Investing* as saying: "A low cost index fund is the most sensible equity investment for the great majority of investors."[154] In a 1993 letter to shareholders, Buffet said, "By

[154] Loudenback, "Warren Buffett Thinks Index Funds are the Best Way for Everyday Investors."

periodically investing in an index fund, the know-nothing investor can actually outperform most investment professionals." [155]

Active Investor

The active investor has a preference for taking on more risk in exchange for the chance at a higher gain. This generally means that this type of investor prefers investing in stocks that are trending upward or specialty ETFs that focus on certain businesses. There are dozens of techniques to help identify investments that could fit this type of investing profile. By using the three tools in section 3 of this chapter, you will be able to identify or at least narrow your investing choices to make a clear decision. For more tools refer to BuildingBread.com/resources.

2. Open the Correct Investing Account(s)

Looking at the primary accounts discussed previously, if you're curious about which one is best for you, it always goes back to knowing yourself as an investor and knowing exactly what your goals are. Your goal will tell you which account to open and what to invest in. If you're looking to invest as much as you can and focus primarily on retirement, then the 401(k) will be your primary account, with either of the IRA options right behind it. If your goal is to invest for retirement but have some flexibility to use the money now, that would be a Roth IRA. For those looking to invest without any limits on how much you can put in and how much can be withdrawn, then a brokerage account would be the best fit. Those looking to save for college, then a 529 plan is the best investing option.

---

[155] Sloan, "Warren Buffett Recommends Investing in Index Funds."

If your goals do not align with the correct account(s), it could prove to be a costly mistake. For example, there are many parents who prefer to offset the cost of their child's education, but using the money from a 401(k) is not the most efficient way to do that and could hurt the entire family's chances at generational wealth down the line. This is because in most situations, withdrawing the money from the 401(k) could result in penalties if drawn before the minimum age and would reduce the ultimate retirement figure and inheritance for the next generation. Instead, had the money been invested in a 529, a student could have paid for college on a tax advantaged basis and left the retirement funds untouched.

3. Find the Right Investments

With your goals and your account aligned, you must now select investments that support those goals and fit the type of account that you have. There are hundreds of different strategies one could use to select their investments; each style is dependent upon experience, risk level, and preference. The following tips are a few suggestions to help narrow down which options might be right for you.

StockComps - an easy-to-use comparison tool that allows you to compare multiple stocks to each other. What I like about this website is that it gives you context and shows you whether the stock you selected beat the index and compares the returns to the amount of money you would have made in a savings account. It's a very good way to visualize the tradeoffs between investing in different stocks, as well as a mutual fund and savings.

Yahoo Finance - an excellent and free tool that allows you to learn more about the market and stay abreast of significant developments with investments. Yahoo Finance also allows you to see how well a company has performed over the years. This allows you as an investor to see exactly how much the company would have made you over a given amount of time.

FinViz – an excellent free stock screen. A stock screener is a tool that allows a user to enter certain criteria. There are more than three thousand individual stocks available in the United States alone and more than seven thousand ETFs available. Unless this is your full-time job, most people aren't able to research thoroughly each of the close to ten thousand investing options. Using FinViz with your selection criteria can quickly narrow and sort dozens of stocks for you, making it easier to dig in and research more of the business information.

4. Avoid the Obvious Losses

There's no way to completely eliminate your risk in the stock market or any investment for that matter; however, there are several ways you can brace yourself if the market falls and a few easy tactics you can use to spot bad investments before deciding to put your money into them. A common phrase in the investing world is that "previous performance does not predict future results." While this is true, the past can provide an important viewpoint on whether or not an investment is worth pursuing. To reduce the impact of losses, it's important to know exactly how well or how badly an investment has performed. This is known as backtesting and it's one of the very first steps I use to determine whether or not an investment is worthy of further research or if it should be avoided for the time being. Backtesting uses historical data to show how an investment would have performed. For Black investors especially, these tactics are important because they help build trust and familiarity in a field that may feel new and complex.

There are dozens of instances where new investors will pour money into a stock without knowing exactly how it's performed in the past and end up losing hundreds, sometimes thousands of dollars. In my view, investing isn't about blindly making the highest amount of money possible. It's more about finding the places that have the highest chance of growing your money. The latter allows you to approach the stock market more as an investor rather than a gambler waiting to get lucky. One prominent example of these two viewpoints played out in July 2020. Kodak, the once famous camera and film company, was trading around $2 per share. Going back to January 2016, the stock had lost 77 percent. This information alone would suggest that there are much better opportunities to grow your money. Comparatively, a company like Apple from January 2016 to July 2020 has gained more than 260 percent. While past performance doesn't predict future results, we do know that one company has a higher likelihood of sustainable growth than the other. Near the end of July 2020, Kodak suddenly spiked more than 1480 percent in just three days to $60 per share due to news that the company received a loan to produce vaccine chemicals related to the COVID-19 pandemic. Within just four weeks the stock price fell below $6. Investors who are blindly seeking profits would have jumped into the stock after seeing such a tremendous gain, and then saw their money evaporate in short order. In contrast, investors who understand how to look at a company's performance history would have been more likely avoid this stock.

Before looking into any investment, it's wise to take a look at the one-, three-, and five-year performance charts. While this is not the extent of your due diligence, this bit of information should give you a good indication on whether or not to research further. Yahoo Finance is a good place to find this information and StockComps also uses historical data.

Another point that you may want to consider when trying to understand your risk is institutional ownership. Between 70-75 percent of all stocks are owned by institutional investors. Institutional investors are usually pension funds, insurance companies, mutual funds, and investment banks. When these large institutions buy or sell a stock, it can have a significant impact on the market because of the amount of money they have. Stocks that generally have large institutional ownership are usually less volatile because these institutions conduct a significant amount of research and have more stringent policies about which companies are added and which companies are sold off. There's no magic number for what the institutional ownership percentage should be, but it's common to see 70 percent or more of a company that's institutionally owned. Companies that are significantly lower than that amount could be a more volatile stock, but it doesn't mean it won't be a good fit for you. With FinViz, you can sort through companies based on their institutional ownership as a way to narrow down your search. Alternatively, you could also do what I call "find hacking" to see what a particular institution is investing in. For example, most mutual funds and ETFs list their top ten holdings, and in some cases they may list every stock that the fund holds. Looking at this list gives you an indication of what that institution is buying and the amount which they are currently holding. Taking the previously mentioned iShares Expanded Tech Stock Sector ETF, the fund is worth $5.7 billion dollars as of January 2021. An amount of 8.5 percent, or $485 million, is invested in Microsoft and it is their largest holding. This tells you as an investor that if this institution believes in Microsoft to such a degree, then it can be a signal for you as an investor that it is a stock worth considering.

If you're looking to invest in individual stocks, your first step should be to use one of the tools mentioned above to gauge how well the company has performed in the past. From there, you may want to consider looking into the level of institutional ownership of that company. If those things line up and you understand the company, you're less likely to have chosen a company that's out of favor or likely to lose a significant amount of money.

5. Invest the Correct Amounts

Now that you have many of the tools to help narrow down potential investment options, you have to decide how much to invest. While 10 percent was the rule of thumb in previous years, 12-15 percent of your pretax income is a better measure. If you receive a company match, this number is included. If you're contributing 10 percent of your income to a 401(k) and your company matches by percent, then you have met the 15 percent goal. For those who may not be able to reach this goal immediately, get as close as you can to the 12-15 percent benchmark and slowly scale up your contributions each year. For someone earning $50,000, they can try to get as close as possible to investing $7,500 each year across their investing accounts. Depending on your situation and the advice from your tax professional, I would prioritize investing in the employer's retirement plan and the Roth IRA as places to start.

The money that's invested will need to be drilled down a bit further. You must then decide how that money is going to be invested each year; this process is called asset allocation. It is the mix between stocks and bonds that you will need to help you reach financial freedom. Those who are younger and have a much longer time frame between now and retirement tend to be more aggressive and have a larger portion of their money in stocks versus the portions they have in bonds. The opposite is true for those who are much closer to retirement. There two key ways to determine this allocation for yourself. The first is the rule of 110. The second is called a risk tolerance questionnaire. The rule of 110 is a shorthand for allocating your investments. Take 110 minus your current age. That number gives you the amount of money you should have in stocks. Someone who is forty years old would have 70 percent of their money in stocks and 30 percent in bonds. For most investors, this 70/30 split is among different index funds. This allows you to help protect and grow your money relative to the time you have to grow that money. If you have a higher appetite for risk, you could choose to invest in individual stocks. The rule here is that you should not have more than 5 percent in any single stock. This too will help manage risk in the event that a stock falls. This is a trade-off; having more money in a high growth company gives you the ability to grow your money significantly, but in most cases you're taking a much higher risk for that type of reward. This 5 percent rule is more of a protection measure, one that helps to buffer your psychological impulses should that investment lose money. (As indicated earlier, studies have shown that losing money is twice as painful psychologically as the joy of making money is pleasurable.)

The risk tolerance questionnaire is a more precise way to reach this number and generally involves answering ten to fifteen questions. You then receive a score that tells you what your allocation should be. At BuildingBread.com/resources, I've included a link to a risk tolerance questionnaire to help you determine how your investments should be allocated. Because of how often the market can move, these allocations don't have to be exact, but they each should be within 5 percent. In most cases anything beyond that 5 percent threshold would need to be readjusted to come back in line with your risk profile. This will be discussed more in secrets number six and seven.

6. Know When to Sell

When you're looking to sell an investment and why you decide to sell both depend on your goals. Someone who's primarily investing for long-term goals like retirement should not be selling those investments on a regular basis in most cases. If you're primarily investing in index funds, there's no real case for selling because we know the history of the stock market and we know that the longer you invest, the higher the chances are that your money will continue to grow and compound. Selling only guarantees that you don't have the opportunity to continue to grow. If you're investing in individual stocks or your investing goals are more short-term, then there are situations where you may want to consider selling and adjusting your investing strategy. Below, I've outlined two scenarios where you should consider selling.

Rebalancing: Rebalancing occurs when you update or adjust your allocation. For example: If someone starts the year with a 70/30 investment mix, it could become an 80/20 allocation based on how the market performed in that year. In a situation like this, you should consider selling close to 10 percent of your stocks and investing that into your bonds. Rebalancing could also occur with individual stocks if they drift well beyond that 5 percent threshold. This helps to ensure that your goals are being reflected in your investing strategy. Rebalancing is something that should happen with all investors on a periodic basis. I will lay out the frequency in which you would rebalance in secret number seven.

A Change in Direction: If there's a major change in direction for a company or a fund and you disagree with that direction, this may be an opportunity for you to consider selling and investing in something that aligns more with your values and strategy. For example, AMC Theatres during the coronavirus pandemic was forced to change directions from their original business model. Companies like Netflix, Disney, and HBO Max have circumvented the traditional theater process so that viewers can watch new movies at home. That's a fundamental shift from the way that AMC was used to operating; it would make sense in this case to sell if you were an investor unless AMC develops an adequate plan or the landscape changes further. For index funds that are focused on a specific sector such as oil or technology, you'll want to pay attention to broader changes that could have an impact on the overall sector, such as a new regulation or innovation that changes how that entire sector is viewed. One good case was the oil and gas sector, when clean technology and green energy was becoming more of a threat. It could have been a good opportunity to sell and move into a space that was more profitable.

I will note that an investment simply falling in value is not reason enough to sell. Every investment at some point in time will take a dip. Sometimes investors will sell out of an investment because it is dropping in hopes of avoiding the pain of loss and try to jump back into an investment at what they feel is the "right time" once things have bottomed out. In most cases, this is a very ineffective way to invest your money. That's because we're not great at timing the market and missing just a few days by sitting on the sidelines can have a negative impact. Since 1999, six out of the ten best days in the stock market always happened within two weeks of the ten worst days according to JP Morgan Asset Management. Missing just ten of the best days in the stock market can cut your performance in half. Data suggest that you're much better off dollar cost averaging through a downturn versus jumping in and out of the market.

7. Set an Investing Schedule

Just like having routine maintenance on a car, you need to have predetermined dates to make adjustments to your investments. This allows you to institute more discipline and control over the moves you make, but it also helps to remove anxiety when dealing with the market. Like the weather, the stock market can move wildly from day to day, but we know from decade to decade that the market tends to rise. Your job is to focus more on the climate rather than the weather.

For most investors, the maximum number of times you should make adjustments to your long-term investing efforts is four times per year. Attempting to make changes on a monthly or biweekly basis does more harm than good. Checking more frequently could lead to what is called performance chasing, which occurs when investors lose patience in their strategy and attempt to make up returns by hopping into riskier investments that may not fit their profiles. My most successful clients opted for biannual or annual reviews. During those appointments, we would rebalance the investing strategy and make any major moves like selling off a stock or ETF and adding a new one.

I'm often asked if one should wait until all of their debt is paid or if they should wait until after the next market crash to start investing. Investing, above all else, is about time, and more time for your money to work and grow will only benefit you. Waiting until all of your debt is paid is a dangerous philosophy. Depending on the level of debt you may have, you may lose several years of compounding interest that you are unable to recover. Your debt is flexible and can be refinanced, and in some cases can be discharged in bankruptcy. There are payment plans and forgiveness for certain types of debt. None of these options are available for those who wait for years to start investing. If you have a significant amount of debt, whether it be credit cards or student loans, it's best to contribute even a small amount to your investments while committing the majority of your funds to paying down the debt, slowly investing more as those debts are paid off. It's important to recognize, especially in the Black community, the relative importance of credit and debt in comparison to other wealth-building factors.

Becoming debt-free is important and can allow you to invest more and become a lot more flexible with the money that you're bringing in. It's not, however, the ultimate measure of financial freedom, nor is having a perfect credit score. Financial freedom is measured by net worth, which is the money you have *after* all of your debts are paid. A high credit score is only a means of acquiring cheaper debt. In fact, obtaining perfect credit is one of the most misleading financial health indicators for generational wealth. It's not an asset that can be passed down via will or beneficiary and its value doesn't compound like real estate or the stock market. Finally, what good is having a net worth of zero when you could pay down your debts and have something left over at the end? Investing is the only way to build wealth; whether it's through the stock market, real estate, or business ownership, Black families must remain hyper focused on building assets and investing to rebuild Black Wall Street.

CHAPTER 11:

GOING BEYOND THE MONEY

Mental health plays an important role in your financial journey. The negative impacts of mental health with regard to financial stress can be amplified for African Americans due to the simple fact that race, wealth, and income are linked. Among all Americans, money is the number one cause of stress. This is because we know that money has the ability to affect every aspect of your life, from the type of health care you receive to the food you eat, the house you live in, and the clothes you wear. There are many that would argue that money isn't everything, that it doesn't buy happiness, but money does buy a level of comfort. In a 2018 study by Northwestern Mutual, 87 percent of respondents stated that "nothing makes them happier" than knowing their money is in a good place.[156] As you're looking to build or maintain your wealth, here are a few areas to consider.

Comparing Your Journey to Others

Humans are naturally social, and with that social need there's a tendency to compare accomplishments, resumes, and personal journeys. It is often quoted that comparison is the thief of all joy

[156] Martin, "Americans Are More Stressed About Money Than Work."

and that it's never wise to compare your first draft to someone's final chapter. All of this is true, and it is something you should keep in mind in every aspect of life.

Your journey is your journey, not to be compared to someone else's. Entrepreneurship, finance, family . . . none of it is a competition. Run your race and stay in your own lane because you may never know the cost that someone else has paid. The more time you spend concerning yourself with the work someone did or didn't do is time you could have spent moving forward. There will always be people who were given more money than you to start their business. There will be people whom you feel do not deserve the credit and accolades that they have. Your only job is to create your financial plan and execute, and that is it.

Overcoming Burnout

When you do anything at a high level that requires attention to detail and sustain such activity for long periods of time, you're at risk for burnout. This isn't only the case for someone looking to build wealth, but it occurs in other areas too. Teachers experience high levels of burnout as well as those in the legal field. If your financial strategy requires you to monitor every transaction or check the market multiple times each day, it can wear you down and lead to burnout. It can also occur if you're not making a dent in some of your larger financial goals. To overcome burnout, many of the same rules apply: a good self-care regimen, a vacation, and regular visits to a therapist can go a long way. In some cases, burnout is simply a result of doing the exact same things to the point of exhaustion, even if those things are successful. If you're feeling burnt out with your finances, it may be time to consider automating or refreshing some of your financial goals. This means that building your savings and other critical areas of your spending take place without requiring you to execute that process. Similar to how taxes are taken from your job, you want to ensure that your savings, bills, and other expenses can be similarly automated. This not only takes the pressure off you but it reduces the time and stress that may come from constantly focusing on your financial situation. The more areas of your financial life that can be on autopilot, the easier things will be and the longer you can sustain those habits. You may also want to consider micro goals or benchmarks to keep you motivated as well. An example of where this works well is paying down large sums of debt. Paying down a $100,000 student loan will feel stressful if you're constantly staring and obsessing over the current balance. Instead, you may remain more motivated by setting benchmarks for every $10,000 that you pay off. Adding this to an automated payment strategy can help take the pressure off of you while also progressing toward the ultimate goal.

Financial Shame

One of the drivers of financial stress is financial shame. Financial shame is made up of many of the social and cultural stigmas that prevent the open discussion about money and the confidence to seek help when needed. Financial shame, especially in the late 1990s and early 2000s, was a popular tactic used by many personal finance experts in an attempt to motivate and push people to improve their financial situation. That tactic had proven to be effective for some, but in today's more complex financial environment, it lacks nuance and compassion to be effective. The financial world has become exponentially more complex than it was a few decades ago.

Massive student loan debt wasn't a financial obstacle the way it is today. Retirement planning was relatively simple because so many companies offered a pension; that's not the case today and learning how to invest on your own is the only way to create financial freedom.

The gospel of financial shame places 100 percent of the blame on the individual, regardless of how complex the situation may be. If you're in debt, it's no one's fault but your own. If you've filed for bankruptcy, the person you should blame is in the mirror. This type of view is overly simplistic and harmful because it takes out the realities of why people fall into debt and what pushes people into dire financial circumstances to begin with. There are some who feel that overspending on luxury items is the cause for massive debt; the truth is that close to 67 percent of all bankruptcies in the United States are due to medical expenses and a loss of income. Loss of income and medical debt alone result in 530,000 bankruptcies each year.[157] Losing a spouse via divorce or separation is also another big portion of how people fall into debt and bankruptcy. These factors are not areas to be shamed over. It's not generally in your control whether or not you lose your job or spouse or have a medical condition with very high expenses.

Overcoming financial shame is a process that should begin with self-inquiry, not only with your relationship with money today but your relationship with money growing up. In 2012, the Association for Financial Counseling and Planning Education found that familial attitudes and habits toward money can predict a person's

---

[157] Himmelstein et al, "Medical Bankruptcy."

financial experience later in life.[158] Whether via self-reflection or the help of a mental health professional, this is a great place to start to understand that relationship and reframe your experiences around money and the actions needed to improve your financial situation.

The next step is to separate your financial situation from your identity. Just because you may be in debt or you haven't yet invested the way you think you should, it does not make you a bad person. It may have been a bad decision, it may have been a bad situation, but you aren't a bad person. Recognize from this point forward that the future is not yet written, and in small steps or giant leaps you can begin moving in the right direction.

Finally, you will need to educate yourself on the best, most efficient ways to move forward. This may include listening to financial podcasts, reading, or working with a professional who understands your goals and has the expertise to help you get there. For more resources and recommended reading, there's a list at BuildingBread.com/resources.

Understanding your financial status from a mental health standpoint is crucial to your individual financial success and the success of the generations that come after you. With these tools at our disposal, it's now time to discuss rebuilding Black Wall Street through community organizing and collective action.

[158] Beutler et al, "New Adolescent Money Attitude Scales."

CHAPTER 12:

ECONOMIC POWER AND STRATEGIC SPENDING

During the research phase of this book, I conducted a small survey asking what people felt was needed to rebuild Black Wall Street in the twenty-first century. I asked about the primary barrier to rebuilding Black Wall Street today and asked for a ranking for what they felt would be the most important solution to further establishing the Black economy. Lack of community was cited as the biggest barrier and sentiments around community investment, financial unity, financial literacy, and business ownership were among the most common responses. We have thoroughly covered the blueprint for personal wealth through the SIP System and the Seven Secrets for Successful Investors. This section will discuss some of the broader community-based tactics to further strengthen the financial status of Black Americans.

Right now, Black Americans spend less than 2 percent of their combined $1.2 trillion income with Black businesses and deposit less than 2 percent of their combined $130 billion of deposits in Black banks.[159] There's evidence to suggest that a more mindful

[159] Rochester, *The Black Tax*, 90.

and purposeful allocation of this money could have an exponential effect on the Black community.

To put those numbers into context, $1.2 trillion in African American buying power supports twenty-four million jobs in the US economy.[160] What is purchased in our communities has a direct impact on employment, which has a direct impact on wealth creation. "If Black Americans moved their $130 billion in deposits to Black-owned banks, those banks would immediately have to hire 31,000 employees across many different departments and spend billions more to upgrade their facilities," says author Shawn D. Rochester.[161] He goes on to say that those banks would then be able to lend $120 billion to foster homeownership, enterprise, and real estate development in the Black community.

Just as they did in Tulsa, we must purposely spend our money with Black-owned businesses whenever possible and deposit at least some portion of our money in Black-owned banks. We must also demand that the businesses we work with also follow this pattern of spending money with Black-owned businesses and depositing money at Black-owned banks as well.

This should be seen as a minimum requirement not only for the small and medium businesses that receive your support but to large multibillion-dollar companies as well. In the summer of 2020, Netflix announced that they would deposit 2 percent of their cash holdings, the equivalent of $100 million dollars, into Black-owned banks.[162] These companies recognize the power of their consumers,

---

[160] Ibid., 103.

[161] Rochester, *The Black Tax*, 110.

[162] Guzman, "Netflix Pledges $100 Million."

that it is within the right of Black Americans to demand more from these larger companies.

It's also important to note the leverage and significance of these types of moves. A company like Netflix is going to have a significant amount of cash on hand sitting in a bank. Simply deciding to move a small portion of that money into a Black bank has nearly no downsides on the company's side (again, the money was going to sit there anyway) and has a monumental impact for these banks and its consumers. These are not new services or expenses that need to be incurred, just redirected.

Black spending can be used as a significant leverage for positive economic and social change. But like any message, it must be targeted to be effective. When breaking down how African Americans spend money, there are some categories where Black spending is overrepresented compared to the total US population. This means significant leverage exists within these categories and should be much easier to see this vision carried out.

African Americans make up 13 percent of the US population but represent 85 percent of all spending in the ethnic hair and beauty aids category, according to Nielsen, at $54 million spent.[163] As a collective, African Americans must demand that the largest suppliers in the beauty and hair category deposit their money with Black-owned banks, hire people in the Black community, and donate their money to Black causes and HBCUs.

This isn't the only category however. African Americans represent 22 percent of the spending on women's fragrances at $152 million,

---

[163] Nielsen, "Black Impact: Consumer Categories Where African Americans Move Markets."

21 percent of feminine hygiene at $54.1 million, and 20 percent of men's toiletries at $62 million.[164] Each of these segments should be encouraged to deposit with Black banks. In total, Nielsen found seventeen categories in which African Americans made up more than 14 percent of the total amount spent, adding up to more than $6.5 billion.

Strategically, this would be a win for businesses and Black consumers. As mentioned, moving money to Black-owned banks can result in more hiring and more capital. For businesses, this level of support can also be viewed as an investment. "38% of African Americans between the ages of 18 and 34 and 41% of those aged 35 or older say they expect the brand they buy to support social causes," according to Nielsen.[165] In the way that smaller, less populated states use the electoral college to strategically flex power, African Americans can use a similar mechanic of bending capital toward Black causes in the areas in which we are overrepresented as consumers.

Strategy is important at the community and political levels as well. To make a real difference, first ensure that as an individual you are using a Black bank in some capacity and buying from Black businesses. Then demand that the businesses that you spend with also commit to depositing their money with Black banks in addition to hiring and supporting Black causes.

"Now the other thing we'll have to do is this: Always anchor our external direct action with the power of economic withdrawal . . . But not only that, we've got to strengthen Black institutions.

---

[164] Cavill, "The Spending and Digital Habits of Black Consumers."

[165] Ibid.

I call upon you to take your money out of the banks downtown and deposit your money in Tri-State Bank. We want a 'bank-in' movement in Memphis . . . You have six or seven black insurance companies here in the city of Memphis. Take out your insurance there. We want to have an 'insurance-in.' . . . We begin the process of building a greater economic base. And at the same time, we are putting pressure where it really hurts. I ask you to follow through here."

Martin Luther King, Jr.
"I've Been to the Mountaintop"
Memphis, 1968

EPILOGUE

It is important to remember that Black history is a byproduct of our collective strategy. I recall how I felt about a story my wife told me after a lecture she attended when were both students at Hampton. It was the first time I learned that Rosa Parks did not simply "happen," nor was she the first Black woman to boycott and be arrested on the Montgomery bus for not giving up her seat. Black leaders had been thinking for years on what to do about Montgomery buses. Nine months before Rosa Parks, fifteen-year-old Claudette Colvin was arrested for refusing to give up her seat for a white person. Colvin's arrest didn't gain the traction that Parks's did, and this was a strategic decision. According to Colvin in 2009, "They didn't think teenagers would be reliable." Colvin also became pregnant and Black leaders at the time also saw her as an "inappropriate symbol for a test case," according to NPR.[166] Parks, age forty-two at the time, was an NAACP secretary, well known, and an experienced activist. In addition to that, "Her skin texture was the kind that people associate with middle class," Colvin said to NPR. Rosa Parks had the right look, one that would endear her to white moderate audiences. Much of the Civil Rights movement was built on strategic framing that purposely displayed how cruel white people, particularly in the South, had been.

---

[166] Margot, "Before Rosa Parks, There Was Claudette Colvin."

One hundred years ago, O.W. Gurley and J.B. Stradford worked together and created a blueprint that impacted more than eight thousand Black men and women in an era when Jim Crow was widely adopted and spreading. What set Greenwood's blueprint apart from other wealthy Black areas like 1920s St. Louis or Atlanta was that Greenwood folks had the opportunity to transform their lives. "It was a place a sharecropper, or ordinary person, could go to have a respectable life, find decent paying work, and hope for a better life for his children."[167] Greenwood allowed for upward mobility more than any other Black district at the time. It allowed parents to send their children to places like the Hampton Institute, Columbia Law School, the Tuskegee Institute, and Spelman College. Shomari Wills, author of *Black Fortunes*, cites that the area had one of the highest Black literacy rates and a high school graduation of above 50 percent, a rare feat at the time. And the Black dollar circulated twenty-six times before leaving the community. Black Wall Street, though, cannot be rebuilt in the same way it was prior to 1921. This doesn't mean that Black people cannot build strong, upwardly mobile communities. Frameworks like the SIP System and the Seven Secrets to Investing Success were created as templates to be applied in any context, regardless of income. They were also created in the same vein as Greenwood, allowing for anyone to build a future in which money is used as a tool to work on your behalf instead of you being used as the primary driver of someone else's wealth.

There will always be those who romanticize the past and wish for this type of overwhelming "unity" and "support" from the Black

---

[167] Wills, *Black Fortunes*, 200.

Wall Street era to return. This line of thinking often ignores the fact that segregation policies often strengthened Black businesses. In the context of today's digital age, this would be significantly more difficult. No longer are people walking into stores, buying groceries, and purchasing items in the same way they did even ten or twenty years ago. The digital age has broadened our buying options and now includes a global marketplace with increasingly more complex items. Across the board, the traditional mom-and-pop business model isn't working.

Today's Black Wall Street will need to adjust to this new reality, one that does not rely on proximity and is nimble enough to adapt in today's environment. To achieve this modern adaptation for Black Wall Street, strategic spending will be an important tool. In the industries where Black dollars are overrepresented, Black Americans can influence how a company operates. This tactic can help advance social and political goals by leveraging buying power in exchange for more targeted and direct investments in Black communities. The SIP System and Seven Secrets to Investor Success can help you build a foundation to create and pass on wealth in ways that will lift up our communities and recreate Black Wall Street for the twenty-first century.

ACKNOWLEDGMENTS

Writing this book is perhaps the biggest professional risk that I've ever taken on. To tell the story of the Tulsa Race Massacre on its own is a tall task. To do so while interweaving the current racial climate with the principles of wealth building, all while releasing the book during the one-hundred-year commemoration as a native son of Tulsa, increased the stakes. I want to first thank all of the incredible authors, researchers, and reporters who came before me, including Randy Krehbiel, James S. Hirsch, Tim Madigan, Hannibal B. Johnson, and Scott Ellsworth. The work of these men not only help me tell the story of Greenwood, but they helped me fill in the blanks of my own personal story and legacy within it.

Thank you to my dad, Kevin Matthews Sr., who provided my earliest memories of Black Wall Street from the books read to my brother and me as kids. This book might not have been possible without that initial spark of curiosity. As an entrepreneur yourself, you allowed me to see the importance of Black businesses and what Black Wall Street could look like today. I'm proud of the steps you've taken as an Oklahoma legislator to tell the story of Greenwood and add our family's name to the history books.

To my mother Janet Lyons and stepfather Barry Lyons, thank you for always giving me the green light to follow my dreams, even when it wasn't easy. To my wife, Jess, thank you for supporting me through this process and pushing me to write this book. Thank for giving me the space to pour myself into research and hack away at my laptop for hours as our kids slept.

Thank you to my mentor, Earl Cox, for taking my calls and believing in my idea enough to introduce me to people who could help me pull this project off. I also want to thank Harlan Landes and Sherrian Crumbley of the Plutus Foundation for their generous support. Thanks to Rockelle Henderson, my book consultant, and Clarence Haynes, my editor, for taking this book and giving it the structure and critical insight that I needed.

Finally, to everyone from Tulsa who's helped me along the way, from teachers to coaches, church family and beyond, thank you.

BIBLIOGRAPHY

"About Probate - How to Probate a Decedent's Estate - The Superior Court of California, County of Santa Clara." How to Probate a Decedent's Estate - The Superior Court of California, County of Santa Clara. The Superior Court of California - County of Santa Clara. https://www.scscourt.org/self_help/probate/property/probate_overview.shtml#cost.

"Black Impact: Consumer Categories Where African Americans Move Markets." Nielsen, February 2, 2015. https://www.nielsen.com/us/en/insights/article/2018/black-impact-consumer-categories-where-african-americans-move-markets/.

"The Creator of Mount Rushmore's Forgotten Ties to White Supremacy." The Washington Post. WP Company, July 2, 2020. https://www.washingtonpost.com/history/2020/07/03/mount-rushmore-gutzon-borglum-klan-stone-mountain/.

"The Essential Guide to Tate Brady: This Land Press - Made by You and Me." The Essential Guide to Tate Brady Comments, August 8, 2013. https://thislandpress.com/2013/08/07/the-essential-guide-to-tate-brady/.

"Felton, Rebecca Latimer." US House of Representatives: History, Art & Archives. https://history.house.gov/People/Listing/F/FELTON,-Rebecca-Latimer-(F000069)/.

"The Importance of Black Doctors." NPR. NPR, July 6, 2020. https://www.npr.org/2020/07/02/886686990/the-importance-of-black-doctors.

"Maine Governor Paul LePage Criticised for 'Racist' Remarks." BBC News. BBC, August 27, 2016. https://www.bbc.com/news/world-us-canada-37204837.

"Prince's Estate Undervalued by about $80 Million, IRS Says." CBS News. CBS Interactive, January 4, 2021. https://www.cbsnews.com/news/prince-estate-undervalued-80-million-irs-says/.

"Tulsa Star." The Gateway to Oklahoma History. Oklahoma Historical Society. https://gateway.okhistory.org/explore/collections/TULSA/.

"Urban Renewal Under Fire." CQ Researcher by CQ Press. https://library.cqpress.com/cqresearcher/document.php?id=cqresrre1963082100#NOTE[1].

Adler, Margot. "Before Rosa Parks, There Was Claudette Colvin." NPR. NPR, March 15, 2009. https://www.npr.org/2009/03/15/101719889/before-rosa-parks-there-was-claudette-colvin.

Albergotti, Reed. "Black Start-up Founders Say Venture Capitalists Are Racist, but the Law Protects Them." The Washington Post. WP Company, July 22, 2020. https://www.washingtonpost.com/technology/2020/07/22/black-entrepreneurs-venture-capital/.

Alsan, Marcella, Owen Garrick, and Grant C. Graziani. Rep. *Does Diversity Matter For Health? Experimental Evidence from Oakland.* National Bureau Of Economic Research, n.d. https://www.nber.org/system/files/working_papers/w24787/w24787.pdf.

Andrews, Brandon. "Here's How Oklahoma's Black Entrepreneurs Are Rebuilding 'Black Wall Street'." Black Enterprise. Black Enterprise, March 22, 2018. https://www.blackenterprise.com/dream-tulsa-black-entrepreneurs-rebuild-black-wall-street/.

American Battlefield Trust. 2021. *The Declaration of Causes of Seceding States.* [online] Available at: <https://www.battlefields.org/learn/primary-sources/declaration-causes-seceding-states#South_Carolina>.

Armus, Teo. "A Chicago Suburb Wants to Give Reparations to Black Residents. Its Funding Source? A Tax on Marijuana." The Washington Post. WP Company, December 2, 2019. https://www.washingtonpost.com/nation/2019/12/02/evanston-illinois-reparations-plan-african-americans-is-marijuana-tax/.

Associated Press. "NFL Anthem Dispute: NFL Commissioner Roger Goodell Fires Back at Trump." NBCNews.com. NBCUniversal News Group, September 23, 2017. https://www.nbcnews.com/politics/donald-trump/nfl-anthem-dispute-trump-says-protesting-players-should-be-fired-n804086?cid=sm_npd_nn_fb_ma&fbclid=IwAR00T07oK-DGWjL-lv81ObskjMzCVnnr1pJ3Hut-ELfH4ExIBPSrRZ5Ij_I.

Berman, Jillian. "One Day after Juneteenth, Trump Will Hold a Rally in Tulsa, Where a Massacre Destroyed 'Black Wall Street' Nearly 100 Years Ago." MarketWatch. MarketWatch, June 20, 2020. https://www.marketwatch.com/story/what-the-1921-tulsa-race-massacre-can-teach-us-about-the-racial-wealth-gap-in-2020-2020-06-19.

Bernard, Diane. "The Creator of Mount Rushmore's Forgotten Ties to White Supremacy." The Washington Post. WP Company, July 2, 2020. https://www.washingtonpost.com/history/2020/07/03/mount-rushmore-gutzon-borglum-klan-stone-mountain/.

Beutler, Ivan F., and Clinton G. Gudmunson. Rep. *New Adolescent Money Attitude Scales: Entitlement and Conscientiousness.* 2 Association for Financial Counseling and Planning Education, 2012. https://files.eric.ed.gov/fulltext/EJ996784.pdf.

Booker, Brakkton. "Excavation Begins For Possible Mass Grave From 1921 Tulsa Race Massacre." NPR. NPR, July 14, 2020. https://www.npr.org/sections/live-updates-protests-for-racial-justice/2020/07/14/890785747/excavation-begins-for-possible-mass-grave-from-1921-tulsa-race-massacre.

Brown, DeNeen L. "Human Rights Watch Calls for Tulsa Race Massacre Reparations a Century after Violence." The Washington Post. WP Company, May 29, 2020. https://www.washingtonpost.com/history/2020/05/29/human-rights-watch-calls-tulsa-race-massacre-reparations-century-after-violence/.

Brown, Dorothy. "How Home Ownership Keeps Blacks Poorer Than Whites." Forbes. Forbes Magazine, December 10, 2012. https://www.forbes.com/sites/forbesleadershipforum/2012/12/10/how-home-ownership-keeps-blacks-poorer-than-whites/#20392b6e4cce.

Bureau of the Census. "Statistic for Oklahoma." www2.census.gov. 1913. [online] Available at: <https://www2.census.gov/library/publications/decennial/1910/abstract/supplement-ok.pdf>.

Cavill, Sarah. "The Spending And Digital Habits Of Black Consumers Present Opportunities For Marketers." DMS Insights, February 24, 2021. https://insights.digitalmediasolutions.com/articles/black-consumers-digital.

Chakraborty, R., 2019. *The massacre of Tulsa's "Black Wall Street"*. [online] Vox. Available at: < https://www.youtube.com/watch?v=x-ItsPBTFO0&t=264s>

Chakraborty, R., 2019. *When white supremacists overthrew a government.* [online] Vox. Available at: <https://www.vox.com/2019/6/20/18693018/white-supremacists-overthrew-government-north-carolina>

Choi, Jung Hyun. "Breaking Down the Black-White Homeownership Gap." Urban Institute. Urban Institute, February 21, 2020. https://www.urban.org/urban-wire/breaking-down-black-white-homeownership-gap.

Coates, T., 2017. *We Were Eight Years in Power*. Random House Inc.

Core.ecu.edu. n.d. [online] Available at: <http://core.ecu.edu/umc/Wilmington/scans/ticketTwo/whiteDeclaration.pdf>.

Crowley, M. and Schuessler, J., 2021. *Trump's 1776 Commission Critiques Liberalism in Report Derided by Historians.* [online] Nytimes.com. Available at: <https://www.nytimes.com/2021/01/18/us/politics/trump-1776-commission-report.html>.

Davidson, Kate. "It Would Take 228 Years for Black Families to Amass Wealth of White Families, Analysis Says." The Wall Street Journal. Dow Jones & Company, August 9, 2016. https://blogs.wsj.com/economics/2016/08/09/it-would-take-228-years-for-black-families-to-amass-wealth-of-white-families-analysis-says/.

DuBois, W.E.B. "Returning Soldiers." The Gilder Lehrman Center for the Study of Slavery, Resistance, and Abolition. Yale University. https://glc.yale.edu/returning-soldiers.

Eji.org. 2017. [online] Available at: <https://eji.org/wp-content/uploads/2019/10/lynching-in-america-targeting-black-veterans-web.pdf>.

Ellis, Maddie. "Pulitzer-Winning Journalist Tells Historically Untold Story of Wilmington Coup." The Daily Tar Heel, February 26, 2020. https://www.dailytarheel.com/article/2020/02/david-zucchino-lecture-0225.

Ellsworth, S., 1992. *Death in a Promised Land: The Tulsa Race Riot of 1921 (Tulsa Race Riot of 1921)*. Louisiana State University Press.

Exhibits.lib.unc.edu. 1898. *"A Horrid Slander."* UNC Libraries. [online] Available at: <https://exhibits.lib.unc.edu/exhibits/show/1898/item/2158>.

Fenwick, Ben. "The Massacre That Destroyed Tulsa's 'Black Wall Street'." The New York Times. The New York Times, July 13, 2020. https://www.nytimes.com/2020/07/13/us/tulsa-massacre-graves-excavation.html.

Fletcher, Michael. "The Country's Last Black-Owned Banks Are in a Fight for Their Survival." The Washington Post. WP Company, April 26, 2019. https://www.washingtonpost.com/news/wonk/wp/2015/02/13/the-countrys-last-black-owned-banks-are-in-a-fight-for-their-survival/.

Fulwood III, Sam. "The United States' History of Segregated Housing Continues to Limit Affordable Housing." Center for American Progress. Center for American Progress, December 15, 2015. https://www.americanprogress.org/issues/race/reports/2016/12/15/294374/the-united-states-history-of-segregated-housing-continues-to-limit-affordable-housing/.

Gara, A., 2021. *The Bezos Of Black Wall Street.* [online] Forbes. Available at: <https://www.forbes.com/sites/antoinegara/2020/06/18/the-bezos-of-black-wall-street-tulsa-race-riots-1921/?sh=798cc9abf321>.

Gates, Eddie Faye. "Reprinting of `Race Riot, 1921' Filling Gaps in Tulsa's History." Tulsa World, July 12, 1998. https://tulsaworld.com/archive/reprinting-of-race-riot-1921-filling-gaps-in-tulsas-history/article_91b1e7f0-ab8b-5a98-8190-ce25e7d2f540.html.

Glass, A., 2021. *All Confederate soldiers gain presidential pardons, Dec. 25, 1868.* [online] POLITICO. Available at: <https://www.politico.com/story/2018/12/25/this-day-in-politics-dec-25-1868-1074077>.

Guzman, Joseph. "Netflix Pledges $100 Million to Support Black Communities in the US." TheHill, June 30, 2020. https://thehill.com/changing-america/respect/equality/505229-netflix-pledges-100-million-to-support-black-communities-in.

Heath, Dreisen. "The Case for Reparations in Tulsa, Oklahoma." Human Rights Watch, October 28, 2020. https://www.hrw.org/news/2020/05/29/case-reparations-tulsa-oklahoma#_Toc41573978.

Heimlich, R., 2021. *What Caused the Civil War?*. [online] Pew Research Center. Available at: <https://www.pewresearch.org/fact-tank/2011/05/18/what-caused-the-civil-war/>.

The Hill. 2020. *Trump says he made Juneteenth 'very famous'*. [online] Available at: <https://thehill.com/homenews/administration/503390-trump-says-he-made-juneteenth-very-famous>.

Himmelstein, David U., Steffie Woolhandle, Robert M. Lawless, Deborah Thorne, and Pamela Foohey. "Http://Ljournal.ru/Wp-Content/Uploads/2017/03/a-2017-023.Pdf." *American Journal of Public Health* 109 (March 2019). https://doi.org/10.18411/a-2017-023.

Hirsch, J., 2002. *Riot and Remembrance.* New York City.

History. 2019. *Red Summer of 1919: How Black WWI Vets Fought Back Against Racist Mobs.* [online] Available at: <https://www.history.com/news/red-summer-1919-riots-chicago-dc-great-migration>.

Hoskin, Maia Niguel. "Black Women Should Be: Believed, Supported, And Paid Equitably. 4 Tips On How To Advocate For Black Women." Forbes. Forbes Magazine, August 13, 2020. https://www.forbes.com/sites/maiahoskin/2020/08/13/black-women-should-be-believed-supported-and-paid-equitably-4-tips-on-how-to-advocate-for-black-women/?sh=302148797484.

Huddleston Jr., Tom. "'Black Wall Street': The History of the Wealthy Black Community and the Massacre Perpetrated There." CNBC. CNBC, July 4, 2020. https://www.cnbc.com/2020/07/04/what-is-black-wall-street-history-of-the-community-and-its-massacre.html.

Kelly, Jack. "A New Study Concludes That It Literally Pays to Switch Jobs Right Now." Forbes. Forbes Magazine, July 26, 2019. https://www.forbes.com/sites/jackkelly/2019/07/26/a-new-study-concludes-that-it-literally-pays-to-switch-jobs-right-now/?sh=335e9c985959.

Krehbiel, Randy, 2019. *Tulsa, 1921.* [S.l.]: Univ of Oklahoma Press.

Krehbiel, Randy. "Race Riot Reparations Questioned." Tulsa World, May 21, 2020. https://tulsaworld.com/archive/race-riot-reparations-questioned/article_6048eda9-4a1c-51fc-b7d4-f554a0bdf8f4.html.

Krehbiel, Randy. "Tulsa Race Massacre: What Happened to Sarah Page and Dick Rowland Following the Massacre?" Tulsa World. Tulsa World , May 31, 2020. https://tulsaworld.com/tulsa-race-massacre-what-happened-to-sarah-page-and-dick-rowland-following-the-massacre/article_67810913-0f34-58da-af38-f6a9ff8ea5e0.html.

Kruse, Kevin M. "How Segregation Caused Your Traffic Jam." The New York Times. The New York Times, August 14, 2019. https://www.nytimes.com/interactive/2019/08/14/magazine/traffic-atlanta-segregation.html.

Levin, Sam. "'This Was Supposed to Be Reparations': Why Is LA's Cannabis Industry Devastating Black Entrepreneurs?" The Guardian. Guardian News and Media, February 3, 2020. https://www.theguardian.com/us-news/2020/feb/03/this-was-supposed-to-be-reparations-why-is-las-cannabis-industry-devastating-black-entrepreneurs.

List, Madeleine. "Providence Mayor Signs Order to Pursue Truth, Reparations for Black, Indigenous People." The Providence Journal. The Providence Journal, July 16, 2020. https://www.providencejournal.com/news/20200716/providence-mayor-signs-order-to-pursue-truth-reparations-for-black-indigenous-people.

Lockhart, P.R. "The 2020 Democratic Primary Debate over Reparations, Explained." Vox. Vox, March 11, 2019. https://www.vox.com/policy-and-politics/2019/3/11/18246741/reparations-democrats-2020-inequality-warren-harris-castro.

Loudenback, Tanza. "Warren Buffett Thinks Index Funds Are the Best Way for Everyday Investors to Grow Their Money - Here's How You Can Start." Business Insider. Business Insider, December 17, 2019. https://www.businessinsider.com/personal-finance/warren-buffett-recommends-index-funds-for-most-investors.

Mann, Carol. "Letter to the Editor: Massacre Too Inflammatory a Description for 1921 Race Riot." Tulsa World, May 13, 2019. https://tulsaworld.com/opinion/letters/letter-to-the-editor-massacre-too-inflammatory-a-description-for-1921-race-riot/article_e9395550-cec9-5fed-84bb-b89e5f0cb6b2.html.

Malito, Alessandra. "Three Reasons You Don't See Many People of Color in the Financial Services Industry - and How to Fix It." MarketWatch. MarketWatch, July 8, 2020. https://www.marketwatch.com/story/three-reasons-you-dont-see-many-people-of-color-in-the-financial-services-industry-and-how-to-fix-it-2020-06-11#:~:text=Zohlen%20is%20speaking%20-specifically%20to,true%20for%20Latinos%2C%20Zohlen%20said.

Martin, Emmie. "Americans Are More Stressed about Money than Work or Relationships-Here's Why." CNBC. CNBC, June 26, 2018. https://www.cnbc.com/2018/06/26/money-is-more-stressful-than-work-or-relationships.html.

Matthews II, Kevin L. "What Is the Racial Wealth Gap and How Can We Fix It?" The Plutus Foundation. The Plutus Foundation, August 3, 2020. https://plutusfoundation.org/2020/racial-wealth-gap/.

May, J., 2021. *Ida Glenn Number One | The Encyclopedia of Oklahoma History and Culture*. [online] Okhistory.org. Available at: <https://www.okhistory.org/publications/enc/entry.php?entry=ID001>.

McDonnell, Brandy. "Watch: '60 Minutes' Delves into the Haunting History of the 1921 Tulsa Race Massacre." Oklahoman.com. Oklahoman, June 16, 2020. https://oklahoman.com/article/5664689/watch-60-minutes-delves-into-the-haunting-history-of-the-1921-tulsa-race-massacre.

Morris, Seren. "What Is Manifest Destiny? The Controversial History of Westward Expansion." Newsweek. Newsweek, July 7, 2020. https://www.newsweek.com/manifest-destiny-history-westward-expansion-us-1515999.

Npr.org. 2012. *1921 Riot Reveals Tulsa's History Of Race Relations*. [online] Available at: <https://www.npr.org/2012/04/10/150335245/history-of-tulsas-race-riot>.

Osborne, Samuel. "Black Women Become Most Educated Group in US." The Independent. Independent Digital News and Media, June 3, 2016. https://www.independent.co.uk/news/world/americas/black-women-become-most-educated-group-us-a7063361.html.

Perlstein, Rick. "Exclusive: Lee Atwater's Infamous 1981 Interview on the Southern Strategy." The Nation, December 7, 2018. https://www.thenation.com/article/archive/exclusive-lee-atwaters-infamous-1981-interview-southern-strategy/.

Peterson, Dana M, and Catherine L Mann. "Closing the Racial Inequality Gaps." Citi GPS. Citi Global Perspectives & Solutions, October 30, 2020. https://www.citivelocity.com/citigps/closing-the-racial-inequality-gaps/.

Phillips, Amber. "LePage Doubles down: 'The Enemy Right Now' Is 'People of Color or People of Hispanic Origin'." The Washington Post. WP Company, April 29, 2019. https://www.washingtonpost.com/news/the-fix/wp/2016/08/26/this-is-gov-paul-richard-lepage-i-would-like-to-talk-to-you-about-your-comments-about-my-being-a-racist-you-expletive/.

The President's Advisory 1776 Commission. Rep. The 1776 Report, n.d. https://ipfs.io/ipfs/QmVzW5NfySnfTk7ucdEoWXshkNUXn3dseBA7ZVrQMBfZey.

Reid, Eric. "Eric Reid: Why Colin Kaepernick and I Decided to Take a Knee." The New York Times. The New York Times, September 25, 2017. https://www.nytimes.com/2017/09/25/opinion/colin-kaepernick-football-protests.html.

Rep. *A Report by the Oklahoma Commission to Study the Tulsa Race Riot of 1921*. Oklahoma Historical Society, n.d. https://www.okhistory.org/research/forms/freport.pdf.

Rochester, Shawn D. *The Black Tax: the Cost of Being Black in America, and What You Can Do to Help Create the 6 Million Jobs and 1.4 Million Businesses That Are Missing in the Black Community*. Southbury, CT: Good Steward Publishing, 2017.

Root, B., n.d. *Policing, Poverty, and Racial Inequality in Tulsa, Oklahoma*. [online] Hrw.org. Available at: <https://www.hrw.org/video-photos/interactive/2019/09/11/policing-poverty-and-racial-inequality-tulsa-oklahoma>.

Ross, Jenna. "The Racial Wealth Gap in America: Asset Types Held by Race." Visual Capitalist, January 25, 2021. https://www.visualcapitalist.com/racial-wealth-gap/.

Samuels, Robert. "Survivors of the Rosewood Massacre Won Reparations. Their Descendants Aren't Sure the Victory Was Enough." The Washington Post. WP Company, April 3, 2020. https://www.washingtonpost.com/graphics/2020/national/rosewood-reparations/.

Sharlet, Jeff. "A Flag for Trump's America." Harper's Magazine. Harper's Magazine Foundation, June 15, 2018. https://harpers.org/archive/2018/07/a-flag-for-trumps-america/.

Sloan, Allan. "Warren Buffett Recommends Investing in Index Funds - But Many of His Employees Don't Have That Option." ProPublica, n.d. https://www.propublica.org/article/warren-buffett-recommends-investing-in-index-funds-but-many-of-his-employees-do-not-have-that-option.

Sidner, Sara. "Minneapolis Police Identify 'Umbrella Man' Who Helped Incite George Floyd Riots, Warrant Says." CNN. Cable News Network, July 30, 2020. https://www.cnn.com/2020/07/28/us/umbrella-man-associated-white-supremacist-group-george-floyd/index.html.

Silva, D., 2021. *What to know about Juneteenth, the emancipation holiday*. [online] NBC News. Available at: <https://www.nbcnews.com/news/us-news/what-know-about-juneteenth-emancipation-holiday-n1231179>.

Souffrant, Jamila. "Journey To Launch: The Black Tax: The Cost of Being Black in America with Shawn Rochester on Apple Podcasts." Journey to Launch. Apple Podcasts, January 29, 2020. https://podcasts.apple.com/us/podcast/137-black-tax-cost-being-black-in-america-shawn-rochester/id1257126028?i=1000463996281.

Stancavage, J., 2019. *Tulsa ranks 18th in income inequality, study says*. [online] Tulsa World. Available at: <https://tulsaworld.com/business/tulsa-ranks-18th-in-income-inequality-study-says/article_06787030-a4e7-56b3-9449-5679132113a7.html>.

State Democratic Executive Committee, The Democratic Handbook, 1898, Documenting the American South, University Library, The University of North Carolina at Chapel Hill, 2002, http://docsouth.unc.edu/nc/dem1898/dem1898.html.

Streshinsky, M., 2021. *Saying No to $1 Billion.* [online] The Atlantic. Available at: <https://www.theatlantic.com/magazine/archive/2011/03/saying-no-to-1-billion/308380/>.

Thompson, Sonia. "Despite Being the Most Educated, Black Women Earn Less Money at Work, in Entrepreneurship, and in Venture Capital. Here Are 3 Ways to Fix It." Inc.com. Inc., August 22, 2019. https://www.inc.com/sonia-thompson/black-women-equal-pay-equity-how-to-make-progress.html.

Tresniowski, Alex. "Burned into Memory." PEOPLE.com, April 14, 2003. https://people.com/archive/burned-into-memory-vol-59-no-14/.

Tsl.texas.gov. 2020. *Juneteenth | TSLAC.* [online] Available at: <https://www.tsl.texas.gov/ref/abouttx/juneteenth.html#:~:text=Texas%20House%20Bill%201016%20passed,parades%2C%20picnics%2C%20and%20dancing.>.

The Tulsa Tribune. "Nab Negro for Attacking Girl In an Elevator." Tulsa World, February 13, 2019. https://tulsaworld.com/archive/nab-negro-for-attacking-girl-in-an-elevator/article_758e0217-1077-5282-bdb9-4eef81f8e12d.html#:~:text=A%20negro%20delivery%20boy%20who,the%20Drexel%20building%20early%20yesterday.

Tulsa-Greenwood Race Riot Claims Accountability Act Of 2007. Subcommittee on the Constitution, Civil Rights, and Civil Liberties Of The Committee On The Judiciary House Of Representatives, 2007. https://www.govinfo.gov/content/pkg/CHRG-110hhrg34924/html/CHRG-110hhrg34924.htm.

Umfleet, LeRae. "1898 Wilmington Race Riot Report ." North Carolina Digital Collections . North Carolina Department of Cultural Resources, May 16, 2006. https://digital.ncdcr.gov/digital/collection/p249901coll22/id/5842.

Umfleet, LeRae. "Alex Manly." NCpedia. NC Office of Archives and History, 2010. https://www.ncpedia.org/biography/manly-alex.

Vigdor, Neil. "North Carolina City Approves Reparations for Black Residents." The New York Times. The New York Times, July 16, 2020. https://www.nytimes.com/2020/07/16/us/reparations-asheville-nc.html.

The Washington Post. 2020. *How the 'Lost Cause' narrative became American history*. [online] Available at: <https://www.youtube.com/watch?v=9Y6luq3aUvc>.

Watson, Kathryn, and Grace Segers. "Trump Blasts 1619 Project on Role of Black Americans and Proposes His Own '1776 Commission.'" CBS News. CBS Interactive, September 18, 2020. https://www.cbsnews.com/news/trump-1619-project-1776-commission/.

Williams, Ward. "Black-Owned Banks by State." Investopedia. Investopedia, February 4, 2021. https://www.investopedia.com/black-owned-banks-by-state-5024944.

Wills, Shomari, 2019. *Black fortunes*. New York: HarperCollins.

Wills, Shomari. "How Race Shapes Retirement Wealth." Investopedia. Investopedia, February 9, 2021. https://www.investopedia.com/retirement-savings-by-race-5086962.

Wilson, Valerie. "Racial Disparities in Income and Poverty Remain Largely Unchanged amid Strong Income Growth in

2019." Working Economics Blog . Economic Policy Institute, September 16, 2020. https://www.epi.org/blog/racial-disparities-in-income-and-poverty-remain-largely-unchanged-amid-strong-income-growth-in-2019/.

Yardley, Jim. "Panel Recommends Reparations in Long-Ignored Tulsa Race Riot." The New York Times. The New York Times, February 5, 2000. https://www.nytimes.com/2000/02/05/us/panel-recommends-reparations-in-long-ignored-tulsa-race-riot.html.

INDEX

CPSIA information can be obtained
at www.ICGtesting.com
Printed in the USA
LVHW030757010621
689025LV00017B/974